# THE KNIGHT FAM
# BRITISH IRON ]

## Laurence Ince

For want of a nail
    the shoe was lost,
For want of a shoe
    the horse was lost,
For want of a horse
    the rider was lost,
For want of a rider
    the battle was lost,
For want of a battle
    the kingdom was lost,
And all for the want
    of a horseshoe nail.
(Traditional Children's Nursery Rhyme)

Ferric Publications
147 Kineton Green Road, B92 7EG. GB.

ISBN 0-9518165-0-0

Produced by Merton Priory Press
Page makeup by Pippin DTP Services
Printed in England by Roebuck Press
Kingston Road, Merton, SW19 1LT

## Table of Contents

## List of Plates



## List of Figures

## List of Tables

# Preface and Acknowledgements.

Many people interested in the history of the British iron industry will be familiar with the name of Knight through the many mentions that the family receive in books and articles. My first encounter with the name was when reading Abiah Darby's account (1779) of the progress her husband, Abraham Darby II, had made in the production of coke iron suitable for forging into wrought iron. She stated that 'Edward Knight Esq. a capitol Iron Master urged my husband to get a patent .....'. To the casual reader it would appear that the many references to the Knight family in journals and books would indicate that the members of the family played an important part in the history of the iron trade. This conclusion is certainly true and yet no complete account of the Knights' involvement in the iron industry has been attempted.

While researching a projected volume on the general history of the British iron industry I decided to spend a few days examining a large collection of Knight family papers and accounts kept at Kidderminster Public Library. I soon became fascinated by the account books of the Knights' Bringewood and Stour Partnerships. The two days' work turned into two years' research. The main accounts stretch from 1726 to 1810 and are summary accounts for the years' business at forges and furnaces. The vast majority of the accounts stretch from one Ladyday (25th March) to the next Ladyday. After 1810 the accounts for the new partnership of John Knight & Co. are far less detailed and end abruptly in 1850.

My task in examining the accounts was greatly facilitated by the work of R.A.Lewis who completed a M.A. thesis in 1949 on the family's activities in the iron industry during the eighteenth century. His must have been a Herculean task as he analysed a large amount of data before the advent of the electronic calculator.

What unfolded from the Knight Manuscripts was a story of the family's involvement in the iron trade which stretched from the late seventeenth century to the early years of the present century. It is a story of innovation and bold decisions. I hope that the reader will find this story interesting, and for my fellow researchers I hope that the appendices will allow them a detailed view of the charcoal iron industry in the eighteenth century and so provide them with a useful research tool.

I would not have been able to complete this study without the patient help and guidance of the reference staff at Kidderminster Public Library. To them I send my many thanks. I must also express my thanks to the staffs of the Worcestershire and Herefordshire Record Offices and to the personnel in the archive department of Birmingham Central Library. I am also grateful to Parkfield Steel Wheels for allowing me access to the present Cookley Works and its records.

# Chapter One

## In the Footsteps of the Foleys.

The charcoal iron industry in Britain during the seventeenth and early eighteenth centuries was dominated by the activities of a family based in the English Midlands. This was the Foley family whose members invested in several iron making partnerships which allowed the family to hold interests in ironworks from West Wales to Cheshire.[1] The principal members of the family included Richard Foley (1588-1657) founder of the family fortune who held numerous ironworks including Hyde Mill, Thomas Foley (1617-1677) the son of Richard who extended the network of Foley ironworks and supplied cannon to the Navy, Robert Foley (1627-1677) brother of Thomas and an ironmonger of Stourbridge, Paul Foley (1650- 1699) who was to rise to become Speaker of the House of Commons and Philip Foley (1653-1716) brother of Paul and described as an ironmaster of Prestwood, Staffordshire.[2]

Foley money and expertise were involved in several of the great iron making partnerships of the late seventeenth century. Two of the most important partnerships were:

(1) "The Ironworks in Partnership" which controlled four furnaces, thirteen forges, four slitting mills and a warehouse. These ironworks were situated in the Forest of Dean, the Stour Valley and as far afield as Pembrokeshire.

(2) "The Staffordshire Works." This partnership controlled Mearheath Furnace, forges at Oakamoor, Consall, Chartley, Bromley and Cannock and slitting mills at Rugeley and Consall.

"The Ironworks in Partnership" was set up in 1692 with the partners agreeing to contribute £39,000 although only £36,277 was finally paid up. Of this total, £21,957 was described as "total debts" and £14,320 as "stock at the works". This partnership consisted of Paul Foley (1⁄6 share), Philip Foley (1⁄6), John Wheeler (1⁄4), Richard Avenant (1⁄4) and Richard Wheeler (1⁄6). John Wheeler was appointed cash holder, in other words, managing director, at a salary of £200 per year. He resided at Wollaston Hall near Stourbridge.

The interlocking Foley enterprises allowed and promoted a pattern of trade which was of great benefit to the iron industry of the English Midlands. Furnaces and forges tended to be spread widely to take advantage of scattered water power sites and the availability of charcoal which was used as the fuel. Pig iron made at the furnaces was converted into wrought iron at the forges. The forges in the English Midlands produced wrought iron (bar iron) mainly for the nailmakers and allied trades of the region. There was a deficiency of pig iron within the region, and much iron had to be imported into the area from other furnaces situated around Britain. It has been calculated that in 1717 central Shropshire and the Birmingham region had a deficiency of about 4,000 tons.[3] Pig iron also had to be imported into the Midlands because the forges made use of two different types of the product. The common type of pig iron was cold short iron which could be made from the typical carbonate ores of the coalfields. The second, more valuable, type of pig iron was tough pig which was produced in the Forest of Dean, the Cumberland - North Lancashire area and Scotland. Using various mixes of these two pig iron types, a whole range of grades of wrought iron could be produced by a forge. Most of the wrought iron turned out by the forges of the Midlands would be of the lesser qualities which would be turned into nail rods at the slitting mill.

"The Ironworks in Partnership" clearly illustrates this pattern of trade which existed in the Midlands at the beginning of the eighteenth century. A reorganisation of the partnership took place at this time when the assets of the group were reduced by a withdrawal from the works in the Stour Valley. These works were taken over by Richard Knight who also became a partner in "The Ironworks in Partnership." So a link between the main group of works and the Stour Valley continued through the presence of Richard Knight in the partnership.

Richard Knight was an experienced ironmaster who brought much technical and business expertise into the partnership. He was born in 1659, the son of Richard Knight of Madeley, Shropshire.[4] His first experience of the iron trade was while working at the Lower Coalbrookdale Forge. He then moved to take over Morton Forge on the River Roden, also in Shropshire. Here he met and married Elizabeth Payne, the daughter of Andrew Payne of Shawbury, a member of a prominent Shropshire family who were involved in the iron industry. As well as forges, Knight also operated furnaces. From 1695 to about 1710 Flaxley Furnace in the Forest of Dean was in his hands, having been acquired from a Foley partnership.[5] Richard Knight also held the Ruabon Furnace in North Wales in partnership with Thomas Lowbridge of Hartlebury. This partnership seems to have ended in 1696 when Richard Knight of Pineton, High Ercall, Shropshire disposed of his share to Thomas Lowbridge.[6] The withdrawal from these furnaces may have been related to Knight's ambitions to increase his Stour Valley holdings. It could also be that operations at Flaxley were given up by Knight after his acquisition and successful operation of a furnace and forge at Bringewood.

The Bringewood Ironworks in Shropshire was leased to Richard Knight in around 1698.[7] The successful operation of this ironworks prompted Knight to purchase the freehold of the Bringewood property in the early years of the eighteenth century. Knight must have had long term plans for Bringewood for most of the other ironworks he operated remained on leasehold. A further furnace was added to Richard Knight's empire in 1712 when he started the production of iron at Charlcotte Furnace situated on the eastern slopes of Brown Clee in Shropshire.[8] This furnace primarily supplied pig iron to the Knight forges at Bringewood and Morton. In 1717 it was assessed that Bringewood Furnace could produce 340 tons of iron each year while Charlcotte could produce 400 tons per year.[9] However, Bringewood did not reach that total because of a shortage of wood.

Richard Knight's interest in the iron industry of the Midlands was further extended by his membership of "The Ironworks in Partnership". By 1710/11 the partnership was divided into the following shares: Thomas Foley - 6, Philip Foley - 3, the executors of Jonn Wheeler - 8, the executors of Richard Avenant - 2½, Richard Knight - 3 and William Rea - 2½. The capital of the partnership was assessed at £27,542.6.[10] It seems likely that at around this time Richard Knight took over the late Richard Avenant's two shares from his executors.[11] Richard Knight was now a member of a partnership which consisted of the most powerful men trading in iron in the English Midlands. However, by 1725 Richard Knight had left the partnership, possibly as a result of the successful operation of his other ironworks and his desire to expand his undertakings in the Stour Valley.

Richard Knight's membership of "The Ironworks in Partnership" had not dulled his appetite for investment in other sectors of the iron trade. Bringewood had become the centre of his ironworks empire, but investment in other works continued. The Willey Furnace in Shropshire was operated in the 1720s by a partnership whose principal member was Richard Knight.[12] He could well have replaced his brother, Francis, in this partnership. The Willey Furnace was operated by a group of investors which included Thomas Green, the executors of Richard Baldwin, Edward Baugh and a member of the Payne family. Edward Baugh was Richard Knight's son-in-law and the Payne family were also related to the Knights through marriage. The Willey partnership was divided into 3200 shares. In 1733 the shares were distributed in the following manner: the executors of Richard Baldwin held 700, Thomas Green held 200, Richard Knight held 1,400, Mr. Payne possessed 400 and Edward Baugh's share amounted to 500. However, Richard Knight seems to have controlled the works with the authority and voting rights of Baugh's and Payne's shares and so nominally held 2,300 shares. Periods of profit and loss seem to have alternated at the Willey Furnace. From Midsummer 1729 to Ladyday 1733 a total loss of £155.6 was made on the production of 505 tons of iron. During this period charcoal cost £2.40 per load and ironstone cost £0.80 per load. There is evidence in the accounts of the Stour Partnership that after the sale of Willey in 1733 Richard Knight was able to sell Willey iron from his stocks until 1740.[13]

Morton Forge in Shropshire continued as part of Richard Knight's iron making network and was being worked as late as February 1723.[14] In the period July 18th 1721 to February 17th 1723 around 328 tons of wrought iron was produced by this forge. Charcoal was bought in at £1.34 per load with the main sources of pig iron being from Edward Hall of the Cheshire Partnership, Madame Boevey of Flaxley Furnace and Richard Knight's own Charlcotte Furnace.

Richard Knight may well have had other forge interests in Shropshire for on the 29th September 1741 he was able to lease to Cornelius and Samuel Hallen property which included Prescott Forge and Hardwick Mill on the River Rea.[15] To protect his own ironmaking interests in the area he leased the property for 5000 years for conversion into a brass and plating works.

Richard Knight's interests in the Stour Valley were further extended when he and his son, Edward, entered into partnership with the owners of Hales Furnace.

This furnace had been operated by Sir Thomas Littleton & Co., but the new company became known as the Stour Partnership.[16] The Knights brought with then into this partnership forges at Cookley and Whittington which guaranteed a market for the pig iron produced at Hales. Richard Knight entered this partnership sometime before 1726, and on Ladyday 1727 the partnership consisted of Sir Thomas Littleton of Hagley Hall (whose stock and money lent totalled £3,565.65), Joseph Cox (£1,100), the executors of Clement Acton (£1,430) and the Knights (£2,000). The story of the Stour Partnership during the 1730s was one of expansion mainly fuelled by the drive and ambition of the Knight family. Richard Knight retired from the iron trade in 1739-40 when he was about eighty years old and his place in the Stour Partnership and at Bringewood was taken by his sons.

Richard Knight certainly seems to have exhibited much drive and enthusiasm in building up his iron making empire. At various times he held a large number of furnaces and forges stretching from the Forest of Dean to North Wales, with considerable holdings in his native county of Shropshire and along the Stour Valley. He was certainly not afraid of switching his resources from area to area and managed to build up a large personal fortune through his iron making activities.

Few personal details of the man have survived although the following story related in the middle of the nineteenth century gives us some clue as to his character:

> *A characteristic anecdote is told of his first competition for a government contract. It was customary then for the government agent to meet the ironmasters at Bristol to let by tender the several contracts for iron, and it had also become the custom for the masters to meet together the night before and arrange amongst themselves for a division of the contracts. Mr. Knight knew all this and resolved to compete himself, but he knew also that he should have no chance at the private meeting. Two days before the appointed time, dressed in his ordinary forge-superintending attire, and mounted on a favourite mare, chosen rather for safety and endurance than for good looks, he set off for Bristol. On the pommel of his saddle was fastened an old nail bag with various pattern nails outside, and behind him was the small valise of the period, which in this instance had seen much service. At the hour fixed Mr. Knight appeared, his tender was accepted, but when sureties were demanded, he said, "There was no one I could ask to be surety, but perhaps the deposit of the money would do as well." "Certainly", said the agent, and from the old nail bag Mr. Knight counted out the guineas on the table.*[17]

Richard Knight's death occurred in 1745, five years after his retirement from the industry he loved and knew so well. He was buried at Burrington below a cast iron gravestone, a fitting memorial to his life's work.

**References.**

1. B.L.C. Johnson, The Foley Partnerships: The Iron Industry at the End of the Charcoal Era, *Economic History Review*, Series 2, 4 (3), 1952, pp. 322-340.

2. Marie B Rowlands, *Masters and Men in the West Midlands Metalware Trades Before the Industrial Revolution*, Manchester, 1975, p. 75.
3. C.K.Hyde, *Technological Change in the British Iron Industry, 1700-1870*, Princeton, 1977, p. 17.
4. R. Page, Richard and Edward Knight: Ironmasters of Bringewood and Wolverley, *Transactions of the Woolhope Naturalists' Field Club*, 43 (1981), p. 8.
5. B.L.C Johnson, New Light on the Iron Industry of the Forest of Dean, *Transactions of the Bristol and Gloucestershire Archaeological Society*, 1953, p. 137.
6. Herefordshire Record Office, (H.R.O.), Hereford, Downton Castle Papers, (D.C.P.), No. 680, Lease release, 29th September 1696.
7. H.G.Bull, Some Account of Bringewood Forge and Furnace, *Transactions of the Woolhope Naturalists' Field Club*, 1869, p. 55.
8. Norman Mutton, Charlcot Furnace 1733-1779, *Historical Metallurgy Group Bulletin, 1966*, pp. 43-53.
9. E.W. Hulme, Statistical History of the Iron Trade of England and Wales 1717-1750, *Transactions of the Newcomen Society*, 9, 1928-29, pp. 12-35
10. B.L.C. Johnson, The Foley Partnership, p. 326.
11. Worcestershire Record Office, Worcester, r899:228 BA 1970, Articles of Agreement, 18th March 1709.
12. H.R.O., D.C.P.,Bundle 431, Miscellaneous Accounts.
13. Kidderminster Public Library. (K.P.L.) Knight Manuscripts, (K.M.), Stour Ironworks Accounts, 1726-1741.
14. H.R.O.,D.C.P., Bundle 431, Miscellaneous Accounts.
15. K.P.L.,K.M., No. 7157, Lease 28th September 1741.
16. K.P.L.,K.M., No. 141, Stour Ironworks' Accounts Ladyday 1726-27.
17. H.G. Bull, op. cit., p. 56.

## PEDIGREE OF THE FAMILY OF KNIGHT, OF SHROPSHIRE AND WORCESTERSHIRE

Richard Knight, of Castle Green, Madeley, Salop.

Francis Knight of Castle Green

Richard Knight of Shawbury and of Downton, Ludlow (1659–1745) = Elizabeth Payne

Richard Knight (1693–1765)

Thomas Knight of Wormesley Grange (1697–1764) = Ursula Nash

Edward Knight of Wolverley (1699–1780) = Elizabeth James

Ralph Knigh (1703–1754)

Richard Payne Knight of Downton Castle (1750–1824)

Thomas Andrew Knight (1759–1838) = Frances Felton

Edward Knight (1734–1812)

James Knight of Ludlow (1735–1808) o.s.p.

John Knight of Lea Castle (1740–1795) = Henrietta, d. of Daniel Cunynghame of St. Kitt's, W.I.

Sir W. E. K. Rouse-Boughton = Charlotte

Thomas Andrew Knight (ob. 1827)

A. J. Rouse-Boughton-Knight = Eliza Severne

C. A. Rouse-Boughton-Knight (1859–1947) = Helen Wilson

John Knight of Wolverley and Simonsbath (1765–1850) = (1) Helen Charlotte Hope Weir (2) Hon. Jane Elizabeth Winn

Thomas Knight (1775–1853) 8 sons and 6 daughters

Frederic Winn Knight K.C.B. (1812–1897) = Florence Marie Couling Gibbs

Charles Allanson Knight (1814–1879)

Margaret = Duke of Sermoneta

Isabella

Edward Lewis Knight (1817–1882) = Henrietta Mary Sanford

Helen Georgiana o.s.p. = Baron Karl von Kanitz

Frederic Sebright Winn Knight (1851–1879)

Charles Lewis W. M. Knight (1863–?)

Lewis Knight, R. N. (1854–1902) o.s.p.

Isabella Dora = W. B. Wasbrough

Eric Ayshford Knight (1863–1944) = Constance Ida Wilson

Guy Cunyngham Knight, Lt.-Col., killed at the Battle of the Marne, 1914 = Menie E. Cro Buchanan

Richard Ayshford Knight (1901–1961) = Hilda Gertrude Gibbons

C.S.Orwin & R.J.Sellick

# Chapter Two.

## The Bringewood Partnership.

The charcoal iron industry of the eighteenth century was made up of several component parts. Pig iron was made at the furnaces and then refined into the more marketable wrought iron at the forges. Sites for the individual furnaces and forges were determined by the availability of iron ore, charcoal and water power. The result of this was that works within a group were often situated at some distance from each other. Pig iron from a furnace often had to be transported great distances over difficult terrain to a forge which would be able to convert it into bar or wrought iron. One of the most important iron making regions in Britain at this time was the West Midlands. In the early eighteenth century the West Midlands produced over 40% of national pig iron output and nearly 60% of bar iron production. The forges in the Birmingham area also consumed about half the pig iron produced in the Forest of Dean.

An important position in the West Midlands' iron industry was occupied by the Bringewood undertakings of the Knight family. Bringewood was a unique works, as the swift flowing River Teme, in its narrow gorge in Shropshire, produced enough water power to sustain the working of both a furnace and a forge. In fact, the Bringewood Ironworks had more of the character of a nineteenth century works with pig iron being produced and then refined into wrought iron on the same site.

The origin of iron making activities at the site lies as far back as the sixteenth century for, in 1584, a lease of Bringewood Forge and farm was granted by Lord Craven to Francis Walker.[1] In 1663 the forge and furnace at Bringewood were leased to Francis Walker who later assigned ownership to his son Richard. A further lease of the Bringewood property was granted in 1690 by William, Earl of Craven, to Job Walker of Wooton, Shropshire. This lease was for a twenty one years term at a rent of £60 per annum.[2]

The Walkers' ownership of the Bringewood Ironworks seems to have ceased in the late 1690s for, in 1698, Richard Knight took a twenty one year lease on the property.[3] One problem, however, stood in the way of the successful operation of the Bringewood Ironworks. This was the difficulty in acquiring the vast amounts of charcoal needed as a fuel for both making pig iron and converting it into wrought iron. The output of iron from the furnace in 1717 was assessed at 340 tons each year, but it had not reached this figure during the year because of a shortage of wood.[4] In the period Christmas 1714 to Ladyday 1719 charcoal for Bringewood was being bought in at a cost of £1.61 per load.[5] It is a possibility that the reason Richard Knight purchased in 1723 the freehold of Leintwardine, the Chase of Bringewood and the Forest of Mochtree was to secure supplies of wood for his ironworks.[6] This, however, did not completely solve the problem for, until the mid-1750s, the pattern of working the furnace at Bringewood was that it was in blast mainly on alternate years[7]. This probably prompted Richard Knight to build a furnace at Charlcotte to supply his forges at Bringewood and Morton with pig iron. The land at Charlcotte was owned in 1620 by Sir Francis Lacon who conveyed the property to James Grove. The property remained for some time in the hands of the Grove family although mortgaged at various times, including once to a member of the Foley family. The property was acquired by Thomas Audley in 1678 and conveyed to Dame Mary Yate, Audley's heir. On the 25th of February 1712 Apollonia Yate transferred the ownership of the land to Richard Knight.[8]

Ironstone for the furnaces at Bringewood and Charlcotte was obtained mainly from the Coal Measure deposits of the Clee Hills. Although semi-retired from the iron trade, Richard Knight was shrewd enough to purchase in 1742 from one Jenks, "all that mountain or waste ground known by the name of Clee Hill, heretofore the property of Somerset Fox, with right of digging for minerals".[9] This augmented earlier leases of mineral rights around the Clee Hills made by the Knight family. In 1733 Richard Knight retired from the management of the Bringewood and Charlcotte investments and leased them to his sons Edward and Ralph. The value of the three works and the mines on the Clee Hills was put at £12,000. Richard Knight transferred £2,300 of his holdings to his third son Edward and £2,795.5 to his fourth son Ralph. The remaining value of the undertakings, about £7,000, was treated as a loan, upon which 4% interest was payable.[10]

On the death of Richard Knight in 1745, the landed estates passed to the eldest son, Richard, who purchased Croft Castle in 1746. The estates were entailed on the male line and Richard had but a single daughter. Thus on Richard Knight's death in 1765 the estates passed to Richard Payne Knight. He was the eldest son of the late Reverend Thomas Knight who was Richard Knight the elder's second son. The Bringewood Ironworks remained in the hands of Edward Knight, but now the operation of the ironworks and the ownership of the land on which it stood had diverged and this was to sow the seeds of a bitter dispute in later years between the two branches of the family.

After Richard Knight had retired from operating Bringewood and Charlcotte the ironworks were managed by his sons Edward and Ralph. Detailed accounts of this partnership's progress are available from Midsummer 1733 to the closure of the works in the late 1770s. Each brother in 1733 held stock to the value of £2,400, and the £7,000 loan was repaid by 1744. Of the original loan, £4,000 was paid back in 1734-35 and £3,000 was repaid at Michaelmas 1744. The partnership prospered and some profits were loaned at 4% to the Stour Partnership. Money was also expended in enlarging the Bringewood Ironworks in 1739-41. After this period of expansion, profits were withdrawn from time to time to keep the capital constantly at about the £20,000 mark.[11]

Ralph Knight resided locally at Bringewood while his brother, Edward, settled at Wolverley, near Kidderminster in Worcestershire. Here, he could control the family's interests in the Stour Partnership and also supervise the sale of Bringewood wrought iron through a storehouse in Bewdley. The furnace at Bringewood was usually out of blast in alternate years during the period 1733-56. However, the furnace was constantly in blast from L.1744 to L.1746 and from L.1747 to L.1749. (L is Ladyday). During the period 1734-50 the greatest output of pig iron in a year was 941.5 tons and the lowest was 123 tons. These figures give a yearly furnace output average when in blast of 560.97 tons. The forge output at this time averaged 358.4 tons of wrought iron each year. Most of the forge production was purchased by Midlands' scythesmiths and ironmongers with lesser amounts going to locksmiths and other manufacturing smiths. This trade accounted for approximately 200 tons of Bringewood's yearly output of wrought iron.[12]

Edward Knight was not only an able merchant but also an innovator. In the late 1730s he began to build a rolling mill at Bringewood in order to enter the tinplate trade. The production of tinplate and blackplate would guarantee a use for large amounts of bar iron produced at Bringewood. Tinplate consists of a thin sheet of iron covered with a thin layer of tin which makes the sheet durable and protects it from rust. This was a German invention, and the early use of tinning was applied to thin sheets of iron produced under the hammer. An early attempt at British tinplate manufacture was tried at Wolverley Lower Mill on the River Stour, but for a variety of reasons the experiment did not meet with success.[13]

A great step forward for the British tinplate industry was taken at John Hanbury's ironworks at Pontypool during the 1690s. Here was perfected the use of a water driven rolling mill to produce thin iron sheets. As well as manufacturing various goods with the sheet iron such as pots, kettles and saucepans, Hanbury also began to produce tinplate. There was an important Midlands' connection with this invention for Hanbury's family originally came from Worcestershire. The use of the rolling process gave British tinplate, "a finer gloss than that made beyond-sea". It also enabled the British makers to produce tinplate more cheaply than the German manufacturers who were slow to adopt the new process.[14] The tinplate market soon began to expand with the product being used to manufacture a variety of new goods including milk churns, cashboxes and tea urns.

It was at this stage that Edward Knight decided to enter the trade. He considered two sites for his new enterprise. The first site was at the Bringewood Ironworks and the second was at the Mitton Lower Forge of the Stour Partnership. The making of tinplate needed large amounts of water for cleaning and driving rolling mills, cheap fuel and a proximity to a supply of wrought iron. Bringewood fitted these conditions well but had one great disadvantage. All the tinplate produced at Bringewood would have to be transported overland along some very rough tracks to Bewdley on the Severn for sale or trans-shipment. Any damage to the tin layer on the plates would render them unsaleable. The transport of tinplates from Bringewood in carts or on the backs of pack horses would have produced a considerable number of reject tinplates. The Mitton Lower Forge, close to the confluence of the Stour and Severn, was ideal for the shipment of tinplate and the import of tin. However, the Mitton Lower Forge was completely utilising all the available water power at the site. Edward Knight decided to compromise by only building the rolling mill at Bringewood which would produce the sheet iron or so called blackplate.[15] This would then be transported to Mitton Lower Forge for tinning. As part of setting up the works, Edward Knight encouraged John Cook II of Stourton Slitting Mill to travel to Pontypool in around 1740 to find out about the Hanbury method of rolling iron and tinning. Cook was one of the principal slitters of iron for the Stour Partnership, and was probably chosen for the task because of a family connection with some of the workers at Pontypool. The Bringewood accounts record the expenditure of £2-10-0 for John Cook's journey to Pontypool. Further details of the tinning process were acquired for the sum of £36-15-0 which is recorded in the accounts for L.1741-42. Just over £192 was spent in L.1739-40 on erecting the rolling mill, and £1,295-15-6 was spent on erecting and carrying on the rolling mill during L.1740-41. The cost in the same year for erecting and carrying on the tinworks was £2,196-8-2. The mill was not just designed for rolling but also could be used for slitting which turned bar iron into long thin rods ready for the nailer to use. The machinery in this building was powered by no less than five waterwheels which brought to eleven the total of waterwheels at the works.[16]

After some initial problems with the tinning process and flooding from the new weir at the rolling mill, an output of over one thousand boxes of tinplate was achieved in L.1742-43. The trade prospered, for just over £520 profit was made by the Bringewood Partnership on their tinplate sales during L.1743-44. The first part of the process would be the rolling of wrought iron into plate at the Bringewood rolling mill. The surfaces of the plates soon succumbed to oxidation thus giving it its name of blackplate. The plate would then be transported to Bewdley and on to Mitton Lower Forge. After unloading the blackplate there would be a return load of iron-rich cinders from the forge for adding to the furnace charges at Charlcotte and Bringewood.

Some blackplate was sold directly from Bringewood but most went to Mitton for tinning. Blackplate was sold and shipped packed in tallow and soft soap to prevent further rusting. At Mitton Lower Forge the blackplate would be cleaned using an acid. This acid was made by fermenting barley 'flower', but also sal-ammoniac was purchased for this operation. The plates would then be immersed in a container full of molten tin - the tin pot. After cooling, excess tin would be removed and the plates polished.

The finished tinplate would then be packed into wooden boxes. Each box contained approximately 225 sheets. No. 1 grade tinplate measured 13¾ in. by 10in. and No. 2 grade measured 13¼in. by 9¾in. The main markets for the tinplate consisted of wholesales to London and Bristol merchants, and local purchases for the Black Country. The tinplate destined for the Black Country would be to supply a flourishing japanning industry.

The use of Bringewood iron for making tinplate assured the brothers of a market for part of their iron production. The Bringewood enterprises continued to make a profit although there was a dramatic fall in the level of these when the furnace at Bringewood was out of blast. In the year L.1748-49 when 752 tons of iron was produced by the furnace a profit of over £1983 was made by the furnace and forge.

The next year saw the furnace out of blast with profits for the furnace and forge falling to just over £290. Difficulty in obtaining charcoal probably dictated this pattern of operation. The deficiency in iron production was remedied by the operation of the Charlcotte Furnace. Small amounts of pig iron from Charlcotte were sold directly to customers, but most of the pig went to the forges at Bringewood and Morton. After the withdrawal of the Knight family from the ownership of the Morton Forge large amounts of pig iron were sold to the forges of the Stour Partnership. In the period 1735-50 Charlcotte could produce on average 402.47 tons of iron in a year. During L.1747-48 the Stour Partnership's forges took the following amounts of pig iron from Charlcotte: Wolverley - 19 tons, Cookley - 5 tons, Mitton Upper Forge - 107 tons, Mitton Lower Forge - 170.9 tons, making a total of 301.9 tons.[17] The pattern of trade saw the main sales of Charlcotte iron to the Stour Partnership being destined for conversion at the Mitton forges. Some of the pig iron produced at the Charlcotte Furnace seems to have been stored at the nearby Bouldon Furnace. Several historians have linked Bouldon to Knight ownership. However, only once was Bouldon iron present at Bringewood Forge and not one of the Stour Partnership's forges ever used Bouldon iron although they regularly purchased Bringewood and Charlcotte pig.

Ralph Knight died in 1754 and the management of Bringewood and Charlcotte fell fully on the shoulders of Edward Knight although he was later helped by his sons James and John. The mid-1750s was an important time for the iron trade with an increase in demand being fuelled by the opening of hostilities in the Seven Years' War. To help meet this demand and to solve the problem of the intermittent working of the furnace at Bringewood, various changes were introduced at the forge. Until this time charcoal had been used as the fuel to change the pig iron into wrought iron at the finery, and charcoal had also been used to reheat the iron in the chafery fire. Edward Knight decided to rebuild the chafery and fire it with coal. He knew from his own experiences that this was possible as all the forges of the Stour Partnership used coal as a fuel in their chaferies, certainly from 1726 onwards and probably earlier than this date. Coal for Bringewood could be easily obtained from the Clee Hills where the Knights already mined iron ore. The consumption of coal in the Bringewood chafery allowed charcoal to be released for use in the furnace. The result of this was that from Ladyday 1756 until Ladyday 1776 the Bringewood Furnace was in blast each year during this period.

During the period L.1756-70 the furnace at Bringewood was producing an average yearly output of 474.6 tons of pig iron with the forge refining an average of 439.2 tons of wrought iron each year. At this time also the output of the tinworks was at a healthy state with 2390 boxes being produced in L.1769-70. Profits from the Bringewood undertakings remained buoyant, ranging from a yearly sum of £554.4 to £3,328.5. This was in marked contrast to the trading account of the Charlcotte Furnace. This furnace had made a profit in each year from L.1733 to L.1747, but intermittent losses had occurred during the 1750s. Much of the pig iron produced at Charlcotte was fined into wrought iron at Bringewood and the forges of the Stour Partnership. During the 1750s the forge at Bringewood operated totally with iron supplied from its own furnace and from Charlcotte. In the 1740s occasional purchases of pig iron for the forge at Bringewood had to be made from other furnaces such as Bouldon and Kidwelly. During the period L.1756-70 Charlcotte Furnace was out of blast during four separate years and losses were made in ten years out of fourteen. These losses ranged from £21.5 to £560.55. The furnace remained active, possibly because the other sectors of the Bringewood Partnership could absorb the losses. Economic conditions at Charlcotte were not bad enough, yet, to envisage closing down the furnace and buying in pig iron from other producers. When in blast, during the period L.1756-70, Charlcotte Furnace produced an average yearly output of 420.6 tons of pig iron. Charlcotte iron was now suffering from the competition of cheaper coke iron which was now able to be easily refined into wrought iron. Economic factors with regards to the supply of raw materials made it difficult for the furnace at Charlcotte even to compete with other charcoal fired furnaces. In L.1756-57 Charlcotte's charcoal was costing £2.80 for each load while charcoal at Bringewood cost £2.23 a load. This price differential remained throughout the working lives of the furnaces and in L.1769-70 Charlcotte's charcoal cost £2.75 for a load while Bringewood was paying £2.40 per load. There was also a problem with the supply of ironstone from the Clee Hills. The mining of ironstone on the Clee Hills had gone on for hundreds of years and the easily won and more valuable ores were becoming exhausted. This drove up the price of ironstone and made iron production at Charlcotte uneconomic. The furnace was only in blast during three separate years in the 1770s before final closure. In L.1770-71 it produced 393 tons of iron, in L.1772-73 the furnace's output was 428 tons and finally in L.1776-77, the output was 575 tons.

The Bringewood Ironworks also faced similar problems to those experienced by the Charlcotte Furnace. In 1766 Edward Knight had transferred half his stock in the concerns to his sons James and John who each then held a quarter interest. Edward Knight continued as a partner until his retirement in 1772 when his share was conveyed to James and John Knight. Edward Knight seems to have chosen the correct time to retire from the Bringewood Partnership for, after 1770, the Bringewood Ironworks faced serious commercial problems with mounting raw material costs. In 1770 a ton of pig iron from Bringewood was valued at £7.75 compared with £7.12 a ton from Hales Furnace and £7 a ton from Aston Furnace. Both Aston and Hales were charcoal fired furnaces making pig iron in the same manner as Bringewood. The price differential had increased by 1777, when a ton of Aston pig iron was valued at £6.10 while the price of a ton of Bringewood pig iron was recorded as £8.98. Coke iron, at this time, could be purchased for as little as £5.79 a ton. During the period L.1772-75 a loss of nearly £1,800 was made on the operations at the Bringewood Ironworks.

The main problem at Bringewood was the supply of ironstone. In 1766 a load of ironstone for Bringewood Furnace could be purchased for £1.05 but by 1775 the price had risen to £1.72. The same period also saw an appreciable rise in charcoal prices. The first part of the works to suffer was the tin mill. Tinplate manufacture ceased in L.1774-75, although some tinplate remained to be sold in the following year. Other tinplate works had been set up in South Wales and the Black Country, and these works had access to much cheaper iron than that available at Bringewood. These developments had priced this pioneer works completely out of the market. Tinplate sales to the Black Country had dropped from 593 boxes in L.1750-51 to 15 boxes in L.1770-71. The furnace at Bringewood was out of blast in L.1776-77 but in the previous year the furnace must have been pushed to its limit to produce no less than 935.6 tons of pig iron. Conditions worsened and the furnace at Bringewood was finally blown out in 1779 although the forge continued to work after this date. In 1780 Edward Knight, the last tenant for life on the lease, died. John and James Knight appeared to be undecided about renewing the lease. The production of iron at Bringewood had certainly become uneconomic but there was a family attachment to the site of Richard Knight's greatest iron working concern. This indecision was a matter of grave concern for Richard Payne Knight, the owner of the Downton Estate on which the works stood.

Richard Payne Knight was the cousin of James and John Knight and was M.P. for Leominster at the time of Edward Knight's death. He had spent much of his youth abroad where he acquired a taste for classical art. His interest in art and his own collection elevated him to the status of being one of the pre-eminent connoisseurs of his day.[18] It has been suggested that Knight, because of his artistic interests, was eager to rid the Downton Estate of the blot of an industrial works on his door step.[19] This was far from the truth. The Downton Estate made a healthy sum from the rent and from selling coppice wood and charcoal to the iron makers at Bringewood. The cessation of production at Bringewood hit Payne Knight's pocket considerably. On the 6th of May 1780 Richard Payne Knight wrote the following to his agent, Samuel Nash:

> *I have this moment received an account of the death of Mr. Knight of Wolverley. You will take possession of the Deepwood etc. as soon as Mr. Thomas Knight can conveniently remove his stock. You will likewise go over immediately to Charlecot and value that farm...Please let me know what you think it worth independent of the Mills and Furnace and also send me the Bringewood Lease.*[20]

At the end of the month he wrote again:

> *I wrote to you last week to inform you that neither of the deeds which you sent me was the Bringewood lease which I now want. I suppose that the lease will decide how long Mr. Knight has a right to keep the forge in order to work up his stock. His excuse for not doing the repairs seems to me a very odd one - however that Business may be deferred till I come into the Country.*[21]

Richard Payne Knight was angered because the working up of the remaining pig iron into wrought iron at the forge seemed to be taking such a long time. He tried to entice James and John Knight into taking a further lease on the property with a view to putting the furnace back into blast. This was declined with James Knight replying that:

*The only ironstone the works can be supplied with for some years will I find come enormously dear and is moreover very lean.*[22]

Matters dragged on for some time and it was not until the Summer of 1783 that Richard Payne Knight took possession of the land and ironworks at Bringewood. On taking control he was horrified to see the dilapidations that had occurred to the buildings. Estimates of repairs were drawn up which amounted to just over £183. The work included the repair of two waterwheels, one of which worked a hammer and the other powered the chafery bellows. The forge buildings needed renovation work which would take 300ft. of rough timber and 15,000 bricks. Richard Payne Knight proceeded with the work in order to attract a tenant willing to take on the running of the forge. The final bill for the repairs came to a little over £311[23].

On completion of the restoration work negotiations were entered into during October 1783 to lease the forge to William Downing of Strangworth Forge, Pembridge, ironmaster; Benjamin Giles of Hope, Shropshire, Gentleman and John Longmore of Cleobury Mortimer.[24] The negotiations did not prove successful and it was not until September 1784 that the forge was leased to Downing and Giles who had been party to the previous year's negotiations. The lease was to run for 31 years with a yearly rent of £114.[25] Richard Payne Knight wisely had a maintenance clause for the buildings written into the lease, and also the lease stipulated that £20 had to be paid for every pheasant or partridge killed on the land. The forge appears to have worked on up to the early years of the nineteenth century.

**References.**

1. H.G. Bull, op. cit., p. 54.
2. H.R.O., D.C.P., Bundles 403 & 598.
   H.G.Bull, op. cit., pp. 54-55.
3. H.G.Bull, op. cit., p. 55.
4. E.W.Hulme, op. cit., pp. 12-35.
5. H.R.O., D.C.P., Bundle 431.
6. H.G.Bull, op. cit., p. 55.
7. K.P.L., K.M., General accounts of the Bringewood Partnership, No. 244-282. All statements concerning profits and outputs made in this paper are taken from the Bringewood accounts. The accounts start on Midsummer 1733 and stretch to Ladyday 1779. Except for the first account all the accounts run from Ladyday of one year to Ladyday of the next.
8. Norman Mutton, Charlcot Furnace 1733-1779, *Historical Metallurgy Group Bulletin*, 1966, p. 48.
   H.R.O., D.C.P., Bundle 703.
9. H.G. Bull, op. cit., P.56.
10. R.A.Lewis, *Two Partnerships of the Knights - A Study of the Midland Iron Industry in the Eighteenth Century*, M.A. Thesis, Birmingham University, 1949, p. 5.
11. R.A.Lewis, op. cit., pp.5-6.
12. Marie B. Rowlands, op. cit., p.69.

13. Peter W. King, Wolverley Lower Mill and the Beginnings of the Tinplate Industry, *Historical Metallurgy*, Vol. 22, No. 2, 1988, pp. 104-113.
14. W.E.Minchinton, *The British Tinplate Industry - A History*, Oxford, 1957, p. 15
15. From the accounts it would seem that the complete production of tinplate took place at Bringewood. Only a close examination of the details of the accounts demonstrate that the rolling of the iron was carried out at Bringewood and the tinning at Mitton Lower Forge. The accounts for the Stour Partnership (K.P.L.,K.M., No. 141-242) show that rent was paid at Mitton Lower Forge for a forge and a tinworks. There are occasional references to the Mitton Lower Forge's tinplate works in the Bringewood accounts such as land tax paid to the Mitton account.
16. H.R.O., D.C.P., Bundle 407, Particulars of what was at Bringewood Forge and Charlcotte Furnace at the time Mr. Edward Knight died, June 11th 1783.
17. K.P.L., K.M., Stour Accounts, L.1747-48.
18. C.S.Orwin & R.J.Sellick, *The Reclamation of Exmoor Forest*, Newton Abbot, 1970, pp. 28-29.
19. Elizabeth Inglis-Jones, The Knights of Downton Castle, *The National Library of Wales Journal*, Vol. XV, No. 3, 1968, p. 250.

20. &
21. Elizabeth Inglis-Jones, op. cit., pp. 250-251.
22. H.R.O., D.C.P., Bundle 431.
23. H.R.O., D.C.P., Bundle 395.
24. H.R.O., D.C.P., Lease 403.
25. H.R.O., D.C.P., Lease 163.

*Plate One* — *Ralph Knight's cast iron memorial slab. This originally was sited in the chancel of Burrington Church in Shropshire and commemorates Ralph Knight's death in 1754, This and other cast iron memorial slabs for members of the Knight and Walker families are now displayed in the grounds of Burrington Church.*

# Chapter Three

## The Stour Partnership.

The Stour forge interests of Richard Knight married to the pig iron production of Sir Thomas Littleton & Co. produced a well balanced partnership with trading links throughout the Midlands. Knight's Stour forges had now been provided with a local producer to satisfy part of their demand for pig iron. Richard Knight would have realised that any expansion by the partnership on the forging side of the business would provide a market for any surplus iron produced by his own Shropshire furnaces.

Richard Knight entered what became known as the Stour Partnership some time before 1726. His initial investment in the undertakings was transferred to his son Edward in L.1726-27, but Richard Knight re-entered the partnership in L.1727-28 when he probably purchased some of the shares owned by Clement Acton who died in about 1725.[1] Acton's shares had been in the hands of his executors for about two years, and this may well have led to some indecision by the partnership until Richard Knight filled the vacuum. By L.1729 the Stour Partnership consisted of the following personnel,

Sir Thomas Littleton with £3,265-13-1 stock and cash lent plus profits for L.1726-29.

Joseph Cox with £1,600 stock and cash lent plus profits.

Richard Knight with £2,500 stock and cash lent plus profits.

Edward Knight with £3,000 stock and cash lent plus profits.

The Stour Partnership united parts of the old Foley business empire with Hales Furnace, and the forges at Whittington and Cookley were combined as one commercial enterprise. Cookley and Whittington were two of a series of forges and slitting mills which had been converted from ancient corn and fulling mills along the Stour. Often more than one mill was converted and joined together to form a forge. Cookley Forge illustrates this development perfectly. In 1649 there were two mills at Cookley, a corn mill built in the reign of Elizabeth I, and a rod or slitting mill. Both of these enterprises were leased by the Sebright family from the Dean and Chapter of Worcester. Before 1693 the corn mill had become a forge sub-let to Richard Wheeler who also occupied the slitting mill. Wheeler was a member of the Foley inspired "Ironworks in Partnership", and Cookley Forge became for a few years one of its producing units. Richard Wheeler apparently became bankrupt in 1703, and the forge passed into the possession of Rebecca Smith, late of Wolverley, who was the wife of John Smith of Amersham, Nottinghamshire, clerk.[2] The slitting mill was let by the Sebrights to Richard Knight who converted it into a forge. Richard Knight then gained the lease of the other forge and united both concerns into a single unit. A further lease for nine years was granted to Richard Knight in 1706 for Cookley Over and Lower Forges. They retained these names on later leases even though they were unified to form one premises.[3]

The Knight family intended to build up their interests in the Stour Valley through the active control of the Stour Partnership. As part of this policy in early 1728 another Stour forge was leased at Wolverley. This forge had originally been two "corn mills under one roof, leased to the Attwood family.[4] In the 1650s the lease was taken over by Joshua Newborough who converted the mills into a forge.[5] Newborough set up the concern with Henry Glover as a partner, but he was later replaced by Philip Foley. After Newborough's death, the forge was leased in about 1695 to Sir Thomas Cookes who transferred it to Talbot Jewkes in around January 1702. A further lease for twenty one years from the Dean and Chapter of Worcester was granted on the Wolverley property to Talbot Jewkes on the 25th of November 1713.[6] The forge was then rented for a short time from 1728 by the Knight family, and in 1731 the lease of the property was assigned from Francis Jewkes, the relict of Talbot Jewkes, to Edward Knight.[7] Leases for the forge were then held by the Knight family from the Dean and Chapter of Worcester until well past the middle of the nineteenth century.[8] The purchase of the Wolverley Forge had been partly financed by loans. The sum of £400 was obtained from W. Cresswell and £600 from Mrs Sarah Clare of Caldwell Castle. These loans attracted an interest payment of 4½% per year.

Profits in the early 1730s were allowed to accumulate and at Ladyday 1733 these were used to increase the partnership's total stock from £9,000 to £13,500.[9] This allowed Mitton Lower Forge to be added to the partnership in 1734 at roughly the same time that Ralph Knight, Edward's brother, entered the business. Sir Thomas Littleton did not appear to agree with this policy of allowing profits to accrue and he withdrew from the partnership at Ladyday 1736. Littleton was replaced by Abraham Spooner and in the following year Joseph Cox retired from the partnership. At Ladyday 1738 the shares of the partnership were held in the following manner:

Abraham Spooner - 3⁄10
Edward Knight - 3⁄10
Richard Knight - 2⁄10
Ralph Knight - 2⁄10

The purchase of Mitton Lower Forge allowed the partnership to increase their production of wrought iron, and in L.1739-40 just over 1414 tons were produced. Most of this iron was slit into nail rods by outside slitters and then returned to the partnership for sale. In the period L.1732-40 wrought iron output totalled 8924.9 tons of which 8236.4 tons were slit into rods. These figures demonstrate that at that time 92.3% of the partnership's output of wrought iron was slit into rods for the nail trade of the West Midlands. From the mid-1730s sales of rod and bar iron ran at over 1000 tons per year.

The inclusion of Abraham Spooner in the Stour Partnership gave the enterprise an expertise in the marketing and selling of iron. He was an ironmonger in Birmingham which meant he bought and sold iron and iron goods, even exporting and importing iron. Spooner was also a member of the Knight family having married Ann Knight, Edward's eldest sister, in 1733.[10]

Further expansion of the partnership's undertakings occurred in 1740 when Mitton Upper Forge was acquired. This site had a very long history indeed, having originally been two corn mills which had been in existence in 1547. They had then been converted into four walke mills and six fulling mills before becoming two forges. The property had descended from John Coote through the Guild of Salters to the Wilmott family of Lower Mitton.[11] The lease of the property was obtained by Richard Knight on the 24th of June 1740, by which time the forges had been united into a single unit. The forge had been operated before this by George Draper of Lower Mitton, ironmaster, John Ingram of Bewdley, gentleman and George Crump of Cleobury Forge.[12] Richard Knight leased the property to the Stour Partnership, with the freehold passing to the Reverend Thomas Knight in 1750.[13] The acquisition of Mitton Upper Forge was aided by the loan of £2,000 from the Bringewood Partnership.[14] The Mitton forges allowed the partnership to greatly increase its production of wrought iron for they were of a larger type than the other Stour forges held by the partners. This additional means of production helped the forges make 1,702 tons of wrought iron during L.1742-43 with a profit of £2,599 being made on the year's transactions. During that year the shares of the partnership were distributed in the following manner:

Abraham Spooner - 3⁄10
Edward Knight - ½
Ralph Knight - ⅕

As well as investing in additional means of production of wrought iron, the partnership also began to purchase foreign iron. This was the Russian Mullers' or Moscow iron. Abraham Spooner was the guiding hand behind this development. Russian iron had been introduced into England in 1715, reaching a peak of importation of 15,000 tons in 1749. Abraham Spooner first began purchasing Mullers' iron in about 1730.[15] The Russian iron was similar to English cold short iron but much cheaper. The Russian iron sold at £11-13 a ton when English rod iron of the same quality sold at £18 per ton. The Stour Partnership began making purchases of Mullers' iron in 1739. During 1741 the partnership bought 267.55 tons of Mullers' iron at a cost of £13.04 a ton and in 1743 the purchases of the Russian iron amounted to 180.65 tons at £12.05 a ton. The yearly purchase of this type of iron varied from 170 tons to 267 tons with slitting taking place initially at the Stour Mills. The purchase of Mullers' iron by the Stour Partnership seems to have died out in about 1750.

The move away from the purchase of Mullers' iron may well have been connected with a period of expansion initiated by the partnership in the late 1740s which increased its ability to produce both pig and wrought iron. The 1740s had seen profits maintained at a fairly high level, and these had not been withdrawn from the partnership. This allowed all the sums of money lent to the concern to be finally paid off in 1745. The sums returned were: £5,400 to Richard Knight, £2,500 to Abraham Spooner, £2,000 to the Bringewood Partnership, and £600 lent by Edward Knight in 1739.[16] Even after settling the debts there was enough money left to initiate expansion by purchasing ironworks near Birmingham which was an important trading centre for the Midlands' iron industry. This initiative must have been taken through the advice of Abraham Spooner who, from his trading base in Birmingham, would have been able to oversee this development. So in 1746 Aston Furnace and Bromford Forge were added to the Stour Partnership. Aston Furnace possessed a long history, having been built sometime before 1615 by Sir Thomas Holte on his own estate.[17] From the late 1630s, the furnace was linked with Bromford Forge which was also situated on Holte land. These properties were in the hands of the Jennens family of ironmasters from about 1638 until the end of the century. They were then transferred to Christopher and Riland Vaughton, and then to John Mander and Phelicia Weaman.[18]

As well as taking control of Aston Furnace and Bromford Forge the Stour Partnership also built a slitting mill at nearby Nechells Park. This was the first time that the partnership had involved itself in the production of nail rods from wrought iron. Until this time the Knights had employed outside slitters to make the rod for the partnership. Most of the slitting mills on the Stour hired themselves out in this way. The erection of the Nechells Park Slitting Mill cost the partnership no less than £1,212-9-0½d. This slitting mill would serve Bromford Forge although it also slit to hire for outside customers. It was at Nechells Park that the partnership's Mullers iron was sent in the late 1740s to be slit, and also the mill was prepared to slit steel for outside customers.

Aston Furnace was the key acquisition in this expansion. The Stour Partnership only owned one furnace situated at Hales, and a second was badly needed to expand their output of pig iron. Hales also had the disadvantage of being a high cost producer of pig iron when compared with other charcoal fired furnaces. During the period L.1740-50 an operational loss was made by Hales Furnace in five of the years, with the furnace being out of blast during three of the years. The yearly average output of the furnace when in blast during the 1740s was 655.5 tons. Aston Furnace appears to have had a greater capacity for iron production, and only attracted an operational loss during two of the first fifteen years of Knight ownership.

Ralph Knight died in 1754 leaving the Stour Partnership completely in the hands of the brothers-in-law, Edward Knight and Abraham Spooner, the most able iron merchants of the family. With Edward Knight positioned in the Stour Valley and Spooner in the great trading centre of Birmingham, they were able to exploit the unprecedented demand for iron in the 1750s. This extra demand had arisen from the opening of hostilities in the Seven Years' War. During the period L.1756-64 sales of wrought iron from the Stour Partnership rose to over 2000 tons a year, and the combined profits for these years totalled over £47,000. The year L.1760-61 produced a profit of no less than £10,617. The demand for iron at this time was high, and large profits could be earned. However, these demand conditions encouraged many people to invest in the fledgling coke iron industry. The enormous demand for iron had also triggered off a large price increase in charcoal. This made charcoal iron the more expensive product compared with coke iron. It was also during the 1750s that the quality of coke iron improved, thus making it readily acceptable at the forges. Moreover, it was at the Stour forges of the Knight family that the large scale use of coke iron for making wrought iron was to be pioneered with Wolverley Forge buying its first coke iron for forging in L.1754-55.

The drop in demand for iron in 1765 saw a considerable reduction in the Stour Partnership's profits. In L.1765-66 profits were only just over £377 compared with the preceding year's profit of £5,286. Sales of wrought iron also dropped to a figure of 1,637 tons. Between L.1760-72 Hales Furnace made a loss in seven years out of twelve, with the furnace out of blast in four years. The cheaper coke iron was now pushing the charcoal furnaces with high input costs out of business. In 1770 a ton of coke iron from the Coalbrookdale Ironworks cost £6.45 with coke iron from the Bradley Ironworks costing £6.20 a ton. Charcoal iron from Hales at the same time was valued at £7.12 a ton while iron from Aston cost £7 a ton. The partnership, which from L.1766 to L.1771 consisted of Abraham Spooner, Edward Knight and his two sons James and John, had to rethink their strategy of production. Edward Knight retired from the partnership in 1771 leaving the business in the hands of Abraham Spooner (6⁄16), James Knight (5⁄16) and John Knight (5⁄16). The partnership decided to close down Hales Furnace in 1772, and the remaining stock was sold off during L.1772-73. However, this had a knock on effect as the partnership's forge at Whittington operated mainly with pig iron from nearby Hales Furnace. Whittington was the partnership's forge which was most difficult to supply with pig iron as it was furthest from Bewdley and the River Severn. Therefore, it was decided to convert Whittington Forge into a slitting mill to serve the remaining forges of the partnership. A licence from the landowner, the Earl of Stamford, to change Whittington into a slitting mill had been applied for as early as December 1770.[19] Whittington Forge became redundant at L.1771, and it took until L.1775 for the slitting mill to be built and set to work. The conversion cost no less than £11,472-12-6¾. It was hoped by the partners that with control of the finishing process for rod iron in their hands profits could be maintained at an adequate level. Profits had dropped to £75 in L.1772-73, and a loss of £786.85 was made in the following year. No doubt the cost of converting Whittington Forge into a slitting mill had adversely affected the balance sheets. Profits, however, recovered and rose to £4618 for the year L.1780-81 although losses by Aston Furnace were still sapping the financial strength of the Knight enterprises. In the period L.1770-84 Aston Furnace was out of blast for five years and losses were made in eight years out of fourteen. The Stour forges were now buying in considerable amounts of coke iron for conversion, and it was decided to blow out Aston Furnace during L.1784-85. The partnership had wisely decided to cease making charcoal pig iron and to concentrate on the conversion of bought in pig iron to wrought iron. With this decision made, profits seem to have recovered to a healthy position. From the time of the closure of Aston Furnace, profits on the partnership's activities did not drop below £1,000 per year until L.1794-95.

The closure of the charcoal furnaces brought about changes at the forges. There was a constant demand for cast iron plates at the forges, and these had been previously produced by the furnaces. To manufacture these plates and produce other castings, foundries were built at Cookley and Bromford. Attempts were now made to widen the range of products manufactured by the partnership. Cookley Forge began to make merchant bar in early 1784, and in L.1789-90 was turned over completely to the manufacture of this higher grade wrought iron. The previous year had seen Abrahan Spooner retire from the concern to be replaced by his son, Isaac Spooner. The ownership of the forges and mills were divided between James and John Knight who each held a 5/16 share, and Isaac Spooner who held a 6/16 share. The entry into the manufacture of merchant bar must have been a decision prompted by the success of the coke iron industry. For at this time not only could pig iron be made with coal, but methods of refining iron into wrought iron with coal had been successfully taken up by ironmasters. The use of the stamping and potting process and Cort's puddling process had revolutionised the iron industry. These methods could produce cheap merchant bar which in turn helped to create new markets for the iron. The Stour Partnership still depended greatly on the nail trade, and in 1792 they acquired the Lower Wolverley Slitting Mill from its tenant, Moses Harper. Other products, however, were also introduced at the mills and forges, for Nash records a visit in 1799 to Wolverley where:

*At the Upper Mill, cannon are bored, this is an ingenious invention, and answers much better than casting them.*[20]

Further changes were to take place after the death of John Knight in 1795. He was replaced in the partnership by his son, John Knight Jnr., and he must have had a most dynamic disposition for he immediately drew up plans to modernise the forges. The reorganisation of the forges was an attempt to fend off the competition of the integrated ironworks which produced pig and wrought iron. The new methods of stamping and potting and puddling were introduced at the Knight forges, and some of the sites were adapted to concentrate on rolling or finishing the wrought iron. It took several years to find the right combination of uses for the forges, but after L.1795-96 there was a great improvement in the Stour Partnership's sales of wrought iron. Sales were at the 1,478 tons mark for L.1794-95, but had risen to 4,020.6 tons in L.1807-08 with profits rising from £1,293 in L.1793-94 to reach £9,476 in L.1805-06.

By 1808, however, it was clear that the forges and mills were crystallising into two distinct operations. One was centered on the Stour Valley, and the other on Birmingham. This, and the death of James Knight, prompted a dismembering of the business. Isaac Spooner, on his own, took over the Bromford and Nechells Park investment. This took some time to organise and it was not until 1812 that John Knight and Isaac Spooner surrendered the leases on these properties.[21] On the 1st of November of the same year Isaac Spooner took a lease for twenty one years of Bromford Forge and Nechells Park Mill.[22] It took some time to share out the assets of the demised partnership, and sales of some of the mills and forges must have taken place for John Knight received as settlement in 1810 a reduced number of Stour forges and mills. John Knight Jnr. now had to face up to the major problem that confronted him. The first option open to him was to sell the properties and invest in the new ironmaking regions, something that, in fact, he had been undertaking since the first few years of the nineteenth century. The alternative was to radically alter the forges and concentrate on the production of iron in his native Stour Valley. He took the latter course and opened up a new and lengthy chapter in the Knight family's involvement with the iron trade of the English Midlands.

**References.**

1. All statements concerning output, profits and make up of the partnership are taken from the Accounts of the Stour Partnership, documents 141-198, Ladyday 1726 - Ladyday 1810, Knight Manuscripts, Kidderminster Public Library.
2. R.A. Lewis, *Two Partnerships of the Knights - A Study of the Midland Iron Industry in the Eighteenth Century*, M.A. Thesis. Birmingham University, 1949, p. 11.
3. The leases for the Cookley property after 1706 are indexed in the handlist of archival material at Kidderminster Library, Knight Manuscripts 7384-7389. However, these documents were destroyed by flooding in the early 1950s. Valuable details of these leases have been taken from the handlist. The leases are also described in, K.P.L., K.M., 7393, the Cookley Arbitration, 11th September 1888.
4. R.A.Lewis, op. cit., p. 17.
5. Peter W. King, Wolverley Lower Mill and the Beginnings of the Tinplate Industry, *Journal of the Historical Metallurgy Society*, Vol. 22, No. 2, 1988, p. 104.
6. K.P.L., K.M., 6427.
7. K.P.L., K.M., 6428.
8. K.P.L., K.M., 6429-6435.
9. R.L.Downes, The Stour Partnership 1726-36, *Economic History Review*, 2nd series, 3, 1950, p. 92.
10. H.R.O., D.C.P., Bundle 262, Marriage Settlement on Abraham Spooner and Ann Knight, 18th June 1733.
11. H.R.O., D.C.P., Bundle 75.
12. H.R.O., D.C.P., Bundle 80.
13. H.R.O., D.C.P., Bundle 80.
14. R.A.Lewis, op. cit., p. 18.
15. Marie B.Rowlands, *Masters and Men in the West Midland Metalware Trades before the Industrial Revolution*, Manchester, 1975, p.63.
16. R.A.Lewis, op. cit., pp. 20-21.
17. Oliver Fairclough, *The Grand Old Mansion : The Holtes and their Successors at Aston Hall, 1618-1864*, Birmingham, 1984, p. 19.
18. Birmingham Central Library, Holte Collection, Leases 18-23 & 88-97.

19. K.P.L., K.M., 7212.
20. Nash, *History of Worcester*, II, 1799, p. 212.
21. B.C.L., H.C., 96.
22. B.C.L., H.C., 97.

Figure Two – The Stour Valley Iron Industry in 1750.

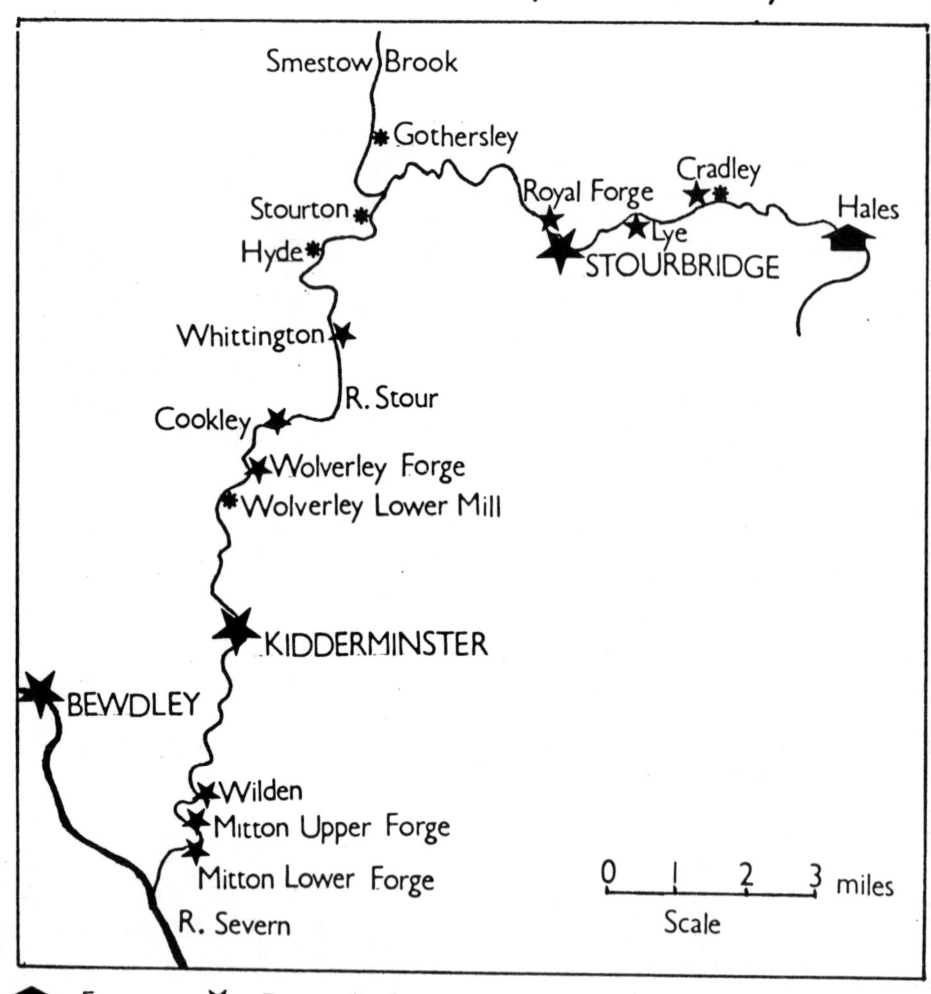

# Chapter Four.

## The Furnaces.

The records of the Knight undertakings allow a fairly detailed examination of the operation of furnaces and forges in England during the eighteenth century. Pig iron was produced by melting iron ore in a furnace and by the eighteenth century the furnace had taken the form of a truncated pyramid approximately twenty five feet in height. The external shape of the furnace was square, but the interior of the structure with its fire brick lining was circular. Charlcotte Furnace has an external measurement of approximately twenty feet square, but the sizes and outputs of furnaces varied greatly. The largest of the Knight furnaces was Aston which, during its ownership by the family, produced a maximum output of 1,041 tons of iron in a year. This can be compared with maximum yearly output figures for the other Knight furnaces. Bringewood produced a maximum yearly output of 941.5 tons with Hales producing 821 tons and Charlcotte 763 tons.[1]

The manufacture of pig iron needs iron ore, a fuel, a flux and a blast of air to raise the burning contents of the furnace to a high enough temperature for the iron ore to melt. The charcoal fired furnace of the eighteenth century was usually blown through a single hole called a tuyère which was positioned in the side of the furnace. The blast of air was produced by a pair of large bellows activated from the cams of a waterwheel. A typical ironworks' bellows was wedge shaped with top and bottom boards made of ash lined with tin or iron, the sides being formed of about 18 bulls' hides. The bellows were 18½ feet long, 2¼ feet deep and 4½ feet wide at the back narrowing down to half that size. However, these bellows were fairly inefficient with much air leaking through the stitches and joints. The leather of the bellows needed a lot of lubrication while working and for this butter and tallow was used. During the 1750s some ironmasters began to use iron cylinders or cylinders and pistons to blow their furnaces. This more efficient method of blowing a furnace greatly aided the development of the coke iron industry, for a higher temperature was needed for the combustion of the fuel. This development seems to have caught the attention of James Knight who patented in 1762 a method of blowing a furnace with pistons working in square blowing tubs.[2] The pistons were powered through a system of chains and levers from a waterwheel. It has been thought that this invention was not a success and was probably never used.[3] However, an inventory of the Bringewood Ironworks for 1780 records the presence of two blast tubs for furnace blowing.[4] It would appear that the degree of success of this invention was enough not to dismantle the machine after its initial use and return to bellows, bur it was not successful enough to adopt at the rest of the Knight furnaces which remained bellows blown. The inventory of 1780 records that Charlcotte Furnace was blown by two large hammer bellows valued at £25 each.[5]

The iron ore consumed at the Knight furnaces came from coal measure deposits. These were ironstone carbonate ores with an iron content of from 12% to 30%. Bringewood and Charlcotte drew their iron ore from the Clee Hills area of Shropshire. At Bringewood the ore price during the period 1733 to 1754 ranged from £0.875 to £1.02 per load. However, the price of ironstone substantially increased to £1.22 a load in L.1756-57, but dropped back after the initial period of the Seven Years' War to £1.07 in L.1758-59. It was to be the 1770s that witnessed a large increase in the cost of Clee Hills' ore with a figure of £1.72 per load being reached in L.1774-75.

Hales Furnace drew its ore from the Black Country, mainly from such localities as Wednesbury, Darlaston, Coseley and Tipton. During the period L.1726-72 the price of a load of ironstone delivered to Hales Furnace varied between £0.59 to £0.90 with a large proportion of the price being taken up with carriage costs. Ironstone costs at Aston varied from £0.62 per load (L.1747-48) to £0.95 per load (L.1778-79). The amount of ore needed to make a ton of iron would vary because of a number of factors. These would include the richness of the ore and the state of the furnace. Often the ore would remain for some time on the ground after mining, and differential weathering would increase its iron content before delivery to the furnace. At Hales the average amount of ironstone needed to make a ton of iron was 2.25 loads and at Charlcotte the average was 2.22 loads.

The operation of an iron furnace during the eighteenth century could be held up for a number of reasons. Lack of water in the stream or freezing conditions could often deny the ironmaster power for his bellows. Renewing the hearth stones or other furnace maintenance could also delay smelting. In 1742 Edward Knight had to obtain a licence from Sir Thomas Littleton, the land owner, before he could proceed with rebuilding Hales Furnace.[6] However, the most important factor with regards to the continuity of working a furnace would be the supply of charcoal. The smelting of iron would require the furnace to be in blast for several days, and a sustained campaign of smelting would require the collection of a large amount of charcoal before the furnace was lit. The charcoal would be kept in a special store or house near to the furnace and treated with great care. The soft charcoal could be easily damaged and small pieces and dust could not be used for smelting. The supply of charcoal was to be the key problem for the ironmaster to deal with each year. In the early days of the blast furnace, wood was cut down in a haphazard way to supply the iron industry. But it did not take long for the landowners to realise that wood could be specially cultivated for the iron industry. Trees could be grown and then cut at ground level to regrow for further cutting after 12 to 20 years. This was the coppicing of wood which allowed the landowner to conserve and reuse the roots of his trees. In 1705 an experienced ironmaster could write the following:

> *The price is risen from 4 & 5s. the long cord to 7 & 8s. the cord. The old woods are most spent but people are generally more careful of their coppice since the encouragement of price. We usually cut at 16 or 17 years*

*growth but if mountain ground and the wood beech then will take 20 years or more. A well grown coppice will yield 12 long cords of an acre if cut every 16 years will make the lands 5s. per acre per annum.*[7]

The cut wood was measured in cords. The long Welsh cord contained 175.5 cubic feet of wood. The standard cord which was the measure mainly used in the English Midlands was 128 cubic feet (8ft. x 4ft. x 4ft.). The cutting of the wood took place during the period 1st November to the 30th March although oak was cut later when the sap was running so that the bark could be sold for tanning. The wood was piled in such a way as to smoulder without complete combustion when set alight. The end product was charcoal minus the impurities contained in the raw wood. The charcoal was stored in, and measured by, the sack. Twelve sacks usually made a dozen or load. However, in the Stour Valley the sacks were larger and eight sacks made a dozen. The data from all the Stour Partnership's works seems to indicate that the Stour Valley load was roughly equal to the load measurement used in the rest of the Midlands. Three and a half standard cords would produce a load or dozen of charcoal weighing 16-17½ cwt.[8]

Bringewood and Charlcotte were fairly well served within their locality for wood. During the period 1733-40 charcoal was being obtained for Bringewood from roughly no further than eight miles away. In 1755-57 there had been a slight increase in the distance that charcoal was travelling to Bringewood, but by 1771-73 charcoal was being obtained from as far as fourteen miles away. Charlcotte seems to have been better placed for wood supplies with the maximum distance of ten miles for the purchase of charcoal not increasing during the life of the furnace. In fact there was a slight contraction to a maximum of eight miles during 1755-57 to return to a maximum of ten miles during the later history of the furnace.

It is rather difficult to work out from the Stour Partnership's accounts the distances that charcoal travelled to Hales Furnace. There is only one brief period where individual locations for the purchase of wood are listed. This listing runs from 1771 to 1778.[9] The accounts list cordwood for both forges and furnace without differentiation. The industrial concerns of the Stour Partnership were so spread out that it makes working out the distances that wood travelled to the furnace or forges rather a lottery. Wood for Hales Furnace and the Stour forges came mainly from the well wooded Stour and Severn Valleys. Localities for the purchase of wood for the Stour Partnership included Hawkbatch, Romsley Hill, the Hagley Estate, Frankley, Alveley, Arley, Ombersley, Lye Hall and Habberley Lodge. Working out the mileages for the supply of wood to the Aston group of works is a little more easy. Wood during the same period was purchased from, near Coleshill (8.2 miles), Shirley (7.1), Knowle (10.25), Cuttel Pool (10.3), West Heath (7), Erdington (4.2), Kingsbury (10.9), Rednal (8.2), Billesley (5.6), Oscott (4.2), Balsall Heath (2.5), Hay Mills Farm (4), Sheldon (6.2), Edgbaston (2.5), Moseley (3.4), Wakegreen Pool Field (3.9), Yardley (4.2), Selly Oak (3.9), Oldbury (4.7), Chelmsley Wood (7.5), Whitacre (11.2), Packwood (12.1), Dogkennel (7.1), Shirley Heath (7.5) and Warley Hall (5.2).

Charcoal consumption at the furnaces varied because of a number of factors. These included the quality of the charcoal, the state of the furnace and the strength and continuity of the blast air. Calculating the consumption of charcoal at the furnaces is fairly straightforward except for Bringewood where charcoal was purchased for use in both furnace and forge. At Charlcotte consumption of charcoal for the production of a ton of iron varied from 1.08 to 2.08 loads, giving an average figure between 1733 and 1777 of 1.73 loads of charcoal consumed to a ton of iron produced. Consumption of charcoal to produce a ton of pig iron at Hales varied between 1.85 and 2.44 loads with an average consumption of 2.12 loads between 1726 and 1772. The figures for Aston vary between 1.77 and 2.09 loads with an average between 1746 and 1780 of 1.96 loads.

The Knight family would have kept a close watch on the charcoal consumption figures for their furnaces and also they would have taken note of the price of the charcoal they purchased. The great disadvantage of charcoal as a fuel was that its supply was inelastic to increase or decrease in demand. Boom conditions in the iron industry might encourage landowners to increase their coppice acreage, but on average it would take sixteen years for those trees to mature for cutting. In times of recession there would be a glut of available wood.

Under these difficult conditions the Knight family operated their furnaces, and much of their time was spent in securing a good supply of charcoal. The price of charcoal had risen in the mid-1720s, but in the ten years after 1728 it had dropped by about a third. In April and May 1736, the woodmasters of the English Midlands petitioned Parliament, asking for a duty on foreign iron. They blamed the import of foreign iron for the closure of some English ironworks and the resultant drop in the price of wood. In 1737 Edward Knight gave evidence to a Parliamentary Committee and stated that he was paying 7s. a cord for wood whereas the price in 1718 was 16s. a cord.[10] At Bringewood the price of charcoal continued to fall until 1744 when a load cost £1.09, then the price began to rise reaching £1.35 a load in 1754. Charlcotte Furnace differed slightly from Bringewood. Here charcoal prices remained steady to increase in the early 1750s to reach £1.90 a load in 1754. At Hales, charcoal prices fell until 1745 when a load of charcoal cost £1.42, then they rose to reach £1.72 per load in 1754. The outbreak of the Seven Years' War saw an increase in demand for iron, with ironmasters trying to obtain extra supplies of charcoal to boost production. The result of this was to produce a large increase in the cost of charcoal. At Bringewood the cost of a load of charcoal in 1754 was £1.35 and this had increased to £2.23 in 1757. Prices at Charlcotte during the same period rose from £1.75 a load to £2.80 and charcoal at Hales rose from £1.72 to £2.14 a load. Aston Furnace costs exhibited a similar phenomenon as the price of charcoal rose from £1.89 to £2.32 a load. The cost of charcoal was the largest input cost in the production of iron and the rise in charcoal prices drove up the price of pig iron. However, the price of pig iron in fact had been moving upwards in the few years before the declaration of war in 1756. In 1750 a ton of pig iron at Hales Furnace was valued at £6.25, in 1754 it stood at £7.00 and in 1758 it had reached £7.87. At Bringewood in 1750 a ton of pig iron was valued £6.00, in 1754 it had reached £6.75 and it rose to £8.00 a ton in 1758. These price increases for charcoal and iron were reversed at all the furnaces in the early 1760s as peace time conditions were restored to the industry. However, the mid-1760s saw a rise in the price of charcoal at Bringewood and Charlcotte which continued into the 1770s and helped make them uncompetitive compared to other furnaces. Prices of charcoal at Aston and Hales tended to remain fairly stable, but even with these static prices the Knight furnaces were becoming uneconomic compared with the new coke fired furnaces. The last Knight furnace to operate was Aston which produced its final batch of pig iron in L.1783-84.

The 1750s probably saw the Knight furnaces producing their maximum output of pig iron. In L.1757-58 the four furnaces produced 2,523 tons of iron which must have been a large proportion of the output of the iron industry of the English Midlands. Even nationally this figure represents about 8.1% of Britain's total iron output.

**References**

1. All output totals and costs are taken from the accounts of the Stour Partnership and the Bringewood Partnership, Knight Manuscripts, Kidderminster Public Library. The Stour Partnership's accounts are yearly and run from one Ladyday to the next. They stretch from 1726 until the dissolution of the partnership. The Bringewood accounts start at Midsummer 1733 but at Ladyday 1734 they become yearly accounts stretching from one Ladyday to the next. The Bringewood accounts terminate on Ladyday 1779.
2. K.P.L.,K.M., 7021, Patent Specification, 1763.
3. *Historical Metallurgy*, Vol. 8, ,No. 1, p. 68.

4. &
5. H.R.O., D.C.P., Bundle 407, Particulars of what was in Bringewood Forge and Charlcotte Furnace at the time Mr. Edward Knight died.
6. K.P.L.,K.M., 7158, Licence granted by Sir Thomas Littleton to Edward Knight to rebuild Hales Furnace, 1742.
7. Gwent County Record Office, Cwmbran, Misc. Ms. 448, Mr. Hanbury's Cost and Yields of Pig, Rod, Hoop and Sheet Iron, page 67, Observations on Woods in Monmouthshire.
8. For discussions on capacities of wood and charcoal see, R.A.Mott, Abraham Darby I and II and the Coal Iron Industry, *Transactions of the Newcomen Society,* Vol 31, 1957-58, pp. 85-86.
G.Hammersley, The Charcoal Iron Industry and its Fuel 1540-1750, *Economic History Review*, 2nd. series, 26, 1973, pp. 603-605.
9. K.P.L., K.M., Cordwood left for the Stour and Aston Works, Stour Accounts 1771-1778, 160-167.
10. R.A.Lewis, *Two Partnerships of the Knights - A Study of the Midland Iron Industry in the Eighteenth Century*, M.A. Thesis, Birmingham University, 1949, p.48.

Figure Three-Aston Furnace in 1758.

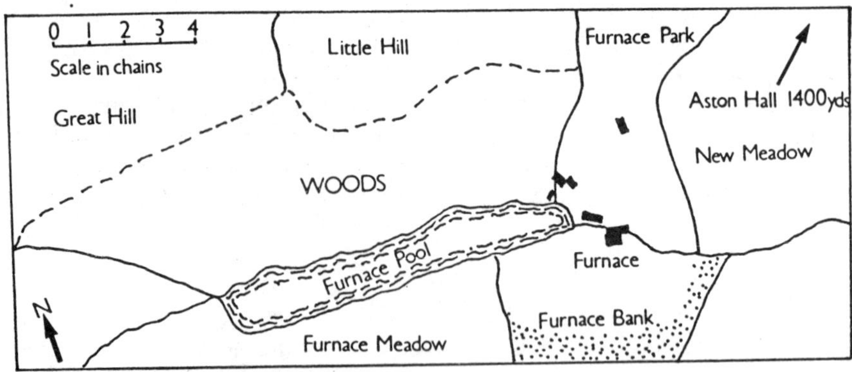


Details taken from 1758 estate map.

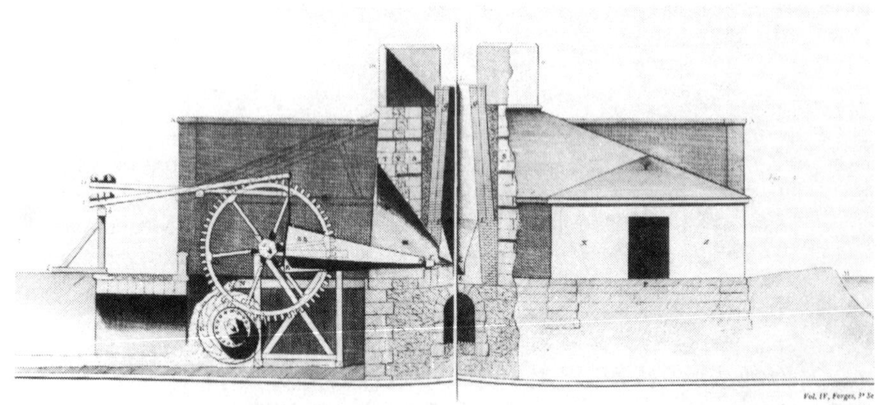

*Plate Two*

*A typical eighteenth century furnace (Diderot's Encyclopedie, photo courtesy of the Ironbridge Gorge Museum)*

*Plate Three* *The present remains of Charlcotte Furnace.*

# Chapter Five.

## The Forges.

The pig iron produced by a furnace was converted into the more desirable wrought iron at a forge. Wrought iron was the commercially pure form of iron. It contained very small percentages of carbon, silicon, manganese and phosphorous. Wrought iron was ductile and could be easily shaped while hot by hammering or rolling. Some shaping of the iron could also be carried out when the product was cold. In the eighteenth century a forge usually consisted of two different hearths called a finery and chafery. The conversion of the pig iron into wrought iron was carried out in the finery. A typical finery measured 5ft. 3in. by 6ft. 3in. and was surmounted by a chimney. The hearth temperature was increased by means of a blast of air directed through a tuyère on to the burning material. The back and tuyère side were closed in by walls. The two opposite sides were left open to allow the finer to work the charcoal fired hearth. The hearth itself had sides of 2ft. 3in. and 1ft. 11in., and was lined with cast iron plates. These plates were set at an angle and this could be varied to adjust the amount of heat to be generated.

The operation at the finery proceeded in several stages. First the hearth was lined with fine charcoal dust and the fireplace filled with charcoal with a pig of iron placed in a suitable place for melting. The pig iron rested on the back or hare plate of the finery. The fire was lit and a blast of air from a water-powered bellows was introduced. The pig iron was then gradually pushed forward over wooden rollers into the hearth. The iron would melt and trickle down in drops. The finer then commenced stirring and working the iron with a long iron bar called a ringer. During the melting the iron would be decarburised. The metal ran to the bottom of the hearth which was cooler and then turned into a semi-solid state. The slag which separated during this operation remained in a slag bath until it reached the level of the slag hole where it was tapped off.

After this first fusion another period of refining took place. The semi-solid iron was broken up, and using an iron cross bar called a furgon or furgeon, those parts that were not sufficiently decarburised were raised towards the tuyère. These were turned upside down and sideways so that all parts were exposed to the blast from the bellows. This was repeated until all parts of the iron were sufficiently refined. Then the last stage of the process commenced. The mass of iron was raised from the hearth bottom and held again in front of the tuyere. New surfaces were exposed to the blast which had been increased at this stage. The iron melted for a third time and formed pasty lumps at the bottom of the hearth. The finer gathered these lumps together into a ball which was termed a bloom or loop. The bloom was a spongy mass of malleable iron whose cracks were filled with slag. The whole process of melting, refining and balling took about an hour.

After the bloom had been made it was taken out of the finery, using large tongs. It was then taken a little distance from the hearth where it was placed on an iron plate. The bloom was then beaten with a large hammer to remove surface charcoal and slag. The bloom was then dragged across the floor of the forge, which was lined with cast iron plates to aid this movement, to a large water-driven hammer. The bloom was then shingled or hammered to force out a fair amount of slag and to consolidate it into a 2ft. square mass of iron. The bloom was then returned to the finery where it was raised to welding heat to sweat out impurities. The bloom was then dragged over the iron-plated floor again to the water-powered hammer to be forged into an ancony. This was an elongated piece of iron, the middle of which was about 3ft. long and bar shaped. Each end of the ancony was left as a thick knob, one being larger than the other. By forging the centre bar part the slag in the iron was driven to the ends.

The process was then completed at the other hearth which was called the chafery. The chafery was similar to the finery except for being slightly larger. This hearth was again lined with cast iron plates. In the chafery the smaller of the two unfinished ends of the ancony was heated for fifteen minutes and then consolidated and forged under the power hammer into the shape of the middle bar. The thicker end, called the mocket head, required two heatings before it was drawn out into the shape of the bar. A higher temperature was required at the chafery to sweat out carbonaceous particles still in the iron. This meant that usually the chafery bellows were larger than the finery ones. The hot iron was finally forged under the hammer into the shape of the bar, and the rough ends cut by chisels.[1]

The fuel used in the finery was charcoal, but the chafery could be fired with charcoal or coal. All the Knight forges along the Stour used coal in the chafery. This required a different design to the chafery compared with one that burned charcoal. Several forges in England attempted to use coal in the chafery but failed; it obviously took different knowledge and skill to work a chafery burning coal to one that burned charcoal. In L.1755-56 the charcoal-fired chafery at the Bringewood Ironworks was turned over to coal firing, and this required a rebuild of the hearth.[2] An important feature of a forge was the cast iron plates which lined the hearths and the floors. These needed frequent replacement and it is no wonder that when the Knights closed down their furnaces it was necessary to construct foundries at Bromford and Cookley.

Output at the forges depended upon the skill of the finer. Often the completion of a stage of refining was identified by the finer through, perhaps, a change in the slag or changes in the colour of sparks. At Wolverley Forge between two and four finers were employed, although four was the usual number. These included John Dudley, Michael Raybold Jnr., Peter Russell and Jeremiah Jackson.[3] The forges owned by the Knight family were of two types. The largest forges were Bringewood and the Mitton forges which each possessed three fineries and a single chafery.[4] Wolverley, Bromford, Cookley and Whittington each had two fineries and one chafery. This difference in forge type is reflected in the following figures for the maximum output for each unit:

| Forge | Output in Tons |
|---|---|
| Bringewood | 525.15 |
| Mitton Upper | 569.00 |
| Mitton Lower | 567.00 |
| Wolverley | 419.50 |
| Cookley | 392.25 |
| Whittington | 351.40 |
| Bromford | 435.75 |

Each of the forges needed a large amount of water power to work hammers and bellows. Bringewood Forge had, at the end of the 1770s, three pairs of bellows at the fineries each powered by a waterwheel. There was also a waterwheel to power a hammer in this part of the forge. Another waterwheel powered the bellows at the chafery along with a wheel to power the chafery hammer. This was in addition to the large waterwheel powering the blowing tubs at the furnace, and five waterwheels at the rolling and slitting mills. This must have represented a huge concentration of water power at one site unequalled by any other eighteenth century ironworks.[5]

It is well known that the English Midlands did not produce enough pig iron to support the forges in its own area. During the period 1726-1801, iron for the Knight forges had to be purchased from over forty different charcoal furnaces, as well as being supplied from their own furnaces. As well as a deficiency of local pig iron there was also a need to blend differing iron types to produce a variety of wrought iron qualities. The two types of pig iron produced by British charcoal furnaces were cold short iron, made by using carbonate Coal Measure ores and tough iron made by the furnaces of the Forest of Dean, North Lancashire and Scotland. The carbonate iron ores could be used to make better quality iron when forge cinder, rich in iron content, was added to the charge. Charlcotte using carbonate Coal Measure ores and cinders from the Mitton forges could supply both ordinary and best grades of pig iron to the Knight forges. The varying types of pig iron could be mixed at the forges to produce different grades of wrought iron. The ordinary grade of wrought iron could be made with cold short iron with a little tough iron added. If the cold short pig iron was a little higher in quality, then 100% of this type could be used to make ordinary bar. This was the grade of iron used by the nail trade and this was the type of iron mainly produced by the Knight forges. The use of larger proportions of tough iron produced wrought iron of a higher grade. The higher grade after ordinary or mill was best, followed by best best, with merchant iron being the highest quality. Merchant bar required a ratio of three parts tough iron to one part cold short iron.[6]

If the major problem for the furnace manager was to acquire adequate stocks of charcoal for smelting, then the forgemaster faced a double problem. Charcoal supplies for the forge would be a problem that was ever present. At Bringewood, where charcoal was used in both finery and chafery until L.1755-56, it took 2.17 loads of charcoal to make a ton of wrought iron at the forge in L.1751-52. The forgemaster also faced the problem of purchasing enough pig iron to feed the finery. This proved to be difficult during boom conditions in the industry. During periods of iron shortages supplies were acquired from some strange sources. Mitton Upper Forge in L.1736-37 bought a small amount of ships' iron ballast squares from the Lloyd family, and in L.1752-53 the accounts for Wolverley show that over two tons of iron which was salvaged from a sunken ship, were bought.

Imported pig iron was also purchased for the Knights' Stour forges. The Knights bought their imported iron from the American colonies. American pig iron was first acquired in L.1728-29 and purchases continued until L.1762-63, although the amount of American iron purchased by the Knights was much reduced after the mid-1740s. The iron was bought from many ironworks including Principio, Potomac, Baltimore, Potuxerant, Tubal, Bush River, Potapsco, Union and Tavioc. There was a close connection between the English Midlands and the American iron industry. Several Birmingham iron merchants had invested in American ironworks and it was those dealers who were mainly supplying American iron to the Knight forges. After L.1762-63 little American iron was purchased, except for a few years in the early 1790s when some American iron was bought from Bristol and London dealers,[7]

As well as buying in pig iron for the forges the Knights made use of scrap iron and broken castings. The cast iron plates used at the forges were replaced regularly, and these discarded, damaged plates were consumed in the finery. The accounts for the forges differentiate between making wrought iron out of pig, and wrought iron out of castings and broken iron. Making wrought iron out of broken iron used up more fuel, and was more expensive in labour charges and thus was accounted for separately. Most of the wrought iron produced by the Knight forges was sent to slitting mills to be turned into nail rods. The slitting mills hired themselves out, and the rods when finished were returned to the forges. The bars from the Knights' Stour forges were mainly slit at Wolverley Lower Mill, Stourton and Hyde with occasional slitting being carried out at Broadwater, Gothersley and Rednal. Slitting a ton of iron during the period L.1731-53 cost £0.75. The pattern of slitting was radically altered when Whittington Forge was converted into a slitting mill in 1775, and later when Wolverley Lower Mill was purchased by the Knights in 1792.[8] This development allowed the Knights to slit their own wrought iron and control that part of the manufacture of nail rods which had been in the outside slitters' hands. The mills acquired by the Knights also hired themselves out for slitting, and in 1796 they were charging at £0.80 per ton.

The Knight forges on the Stour were visited in September 1754 by the ironmaster Charles Wood, who recorded the following in his diary:

> *We then came to Whittington forge, belonging to Mr.Knight. This is a double work & refinery & a chafery which make from English pigs from 7 to 8 ton weekly, if they have water, but never less than 300 tons per Annum. They draw out with pit coal and get ½ cwt. yield. The next place was Cookley forge belonging to the same person, works in the same order*

*& make the same quantity, draw out with pit coal, yield ½ cwt. Their hammer about 6 cwt. does but slow, yet draws 10 Ton weekly when they have Water. Below this, there is a hammermans forge, it was not at Work. The Hammer wheel is out 8½ feet diameter, head and fall about 6 feet. The next forge was Wolverley, a Double work, belonging to the same person. They work all foreign pigs, one finery with Tubal & Cardiff pigs for Mill Iron, the other with Bush River pigs for Mill best tough, they say makes the best iron in England. I know it to be good pig. The make of blend 3½ ton and of B.B. 3 ton weekly. They draw both sorts with pit coal & have ½ cwt. on the Ton thro' the year.*

*Their blooms or anchonies go at 20 to the Ton. Their barrs are a full inch thick. They give 11s. per ton for Anchonies Doublehand, if they make 3 ton, if less but 10s. 6d. For drawing 9d. & 1d. per cwt. over yield. But to keep up quantity, I am informed that if the finer cannot keep to 3 ton per week, Mr. Knight will not keep him, but this does not often happen. There is not any Clerk at any of these forges. The stocktaker keeps an Account and delivers it once a Week to one of Mr. Knight's Sons. They use 11 sacks of Coals for 1 Ton of Blooms, 8 sacks to the dozen. A Sack is 2½ yards long & 4 feet wide.*[9]

Some of Wood's comments, however, are misleading. The description of Wolverley Forge's output must be examined very carefully. He uses the term foreign pig iron but he must mean iron bought from outside the local area. The accounts for Wolverley Forge for L.1754-55 inform us that during the year only 8 tons of Bush River pigs were purchased for the forge and 33.60 tons of Tubal pigs were bought. At the same time 189 tons of Welsh pigs, 100 tons of Aston pigs, 3 of Hales, 20 of Leighton and a further 14.90 tons of Baltimore pigs were bought. The figures seem to indicate that Wood saw an isolated week and not something that was the normal pattern of production at the forge. It would appear that the figures demonstrate that the overwhelming output from the forge was mill or ordinary wrought iron.

The Stour forges of the Knight family occupy an important place in the story of the development of the British iron industry. It was at these forges in the mid-1750s that the large scale conversion of coke iron into wrought iron was initiated.

The use of coke as a fuel for smelting iron was pioneered in around 1709 by Abraham Darby at the Coalbrookdale Ironworks. This venture was an economic success as using coke as a fuel produced an iron well suited to the casting trade, and it was this trade that Darby wished to exploit. Although the Coalbrookdale Ironworks prospered, few ironmasters showed an interest in making coke iron until the 1750s. Why did it take so long for this innovation to spread through the industry? Ashton answered this question in his classic history of the iron trade. He came to the conclusion that the quality of the iron produced at Coalbrookdale was not good enough for use at the forges for conversion into wrought iron. A technical breakthrough had to be made to improve the quality and this happened in the early 1750s. To support this theory the following letter was quoted. This was written in 1779 by Abiah Darby, the wife of Abraham Darby II:

*...about 26 years ago my Husband conceived this happy thought - that it might be possible to make bar from pit coal pigs - upon this he sent some of our pigs to be tryed at the Forges, and that no prejudice might arise against them, he did not discover from whence they came, or of what quality they were. And good account being given of their working, he errected Blast Furnaces for pig iron for Forges - Edward Knight Esqr. a capitol Iron Master urged my Husband to get a patent, that he might reap the benefit for years of this happy discovery: but he said he would not deprive the publick of Such an Acquisition which he was Satisfyed it would be; and so it proved.*[10]

So Abiah Darby dates her husband's innovation to around 1753. This discovery was supposed to have improved the quality of the coke iron in respect of forge use. This 'quality of iron' theory was then accepted as the main reason for the retardation of the spread of making iron with coke as the fuel. Until the 1970s this was the version accepted by most historians although the innovation pioneered by Abraham Darby II was never pinned down and described.

However, this acceptance of the 'quality of iron' theory was rebutted by the work of C.K.Hyde in the 1970s.[11] His thought provoking work was based on the examination of the accounts of furnaces and forges and opened up what could be called the 'Great Coke Iron Debate'. He came to the conclusion that it was the price differential between the relatively cheap coke iron and the more expensive charcoal iron that triggered off the spread of making coke iron. This differential was supposed to have been reached in the mid-1750s. This theory was based on the figures from the forge at Coalbrookdale where coke iron was used exclusively to produce bar or wrought iron in the period 1732 to 1738. The use of coke iron during this period at a forge was explained away by historians who believed that the quality of wrought iron produced was not good and so its use died out. However, six years seems a long time to have taken to come to that decision. The figures from Coalbrookdale for this period show that it took 1.41 tons of pig iron and 3.06 dozens or loads of charcoal to make 1 ton of wrought iron (bar).[12] The charcoal was used to fire the finery while coal was used in the chafery. Hyde compared these figures with other forges which operated using charcoal iron. He found that the Coalbrookdale Forge figures were high compared with other contemporary forges. He then transferred the Coalbrookdale figures to a Yorkshire forge (Colnbridge) with a fairly low consumption of fuel and pig iron. The result of these calculations was that Hyde felt that coke iron would only have been adopted at Colnbridge if it was definitely £1 a ton cheaper than charcoal iron and he even believed that a £2 a ton differential was more realistic. This 'price theory' was generally accepted and now holds sway over the 'quality of iron' theory.[13]

The outlines of these differing ideas have been recently explored by Harris in his review of the history of the British iron industry 1700-1850. Although accepting Hyde's theory Harris does point out that,

*The almost headlong development of new furnaces at Horsehay and Ketley by the normally cautious Darby partners, already determined on*

*by 1753 in the face of scepticism and expectation of their ruin by local industrialists, support those who would still claim some significant technological strides in the Severn Gorge about 1750.*[14]

There are, however, certain inconsistent statements made by Hyde in his book. A total charcoal consumption for the Coalbrookdale Forge (3.5 to 4 loads) had to be estimated because coal was used in the chafery. Hyde explains this in the following terms, "charcoal consumption cannot be readily compared to that of other forges because coal was used instead of charcoal in the chafery fire".[15] Yet Hyde had inspected the Knight accounts of their Stour forges and used figures for iron and charcoal costs from them in his thesis. Even as early as the 1720s the Knights' forges were using coal as a fuel in the chafery. His argument concerning the adoption of coke iron which hinges on a large price differential between coke and charcoal is not well supported. The only evidence submitted by Hyde for this differential is a graph of iron prices for three ironworks taken from a 1949 thesis.[16]

First use of coke pig iron by the forges of the Stour Partnership was between Ladyday 1754 and Ladyday 1755. Introduction of coke iron took place at Wolverley Forge when 6 tons of Coalbrookdale iron was purchased from an independent dealer. Wolverley Forge had a maximum output of just over 300 tons of mainly ordinary bar. It is not surprising that Wolverley was the first of the Knights' forges to try coke iron for this was the centre of their business empire with Edward Knight living in close proximity to the forge. In the next year nearly 111 tons of coke iron was purchased for Wolverley, 64 tons for Cookley and 79 tons for Whittington. All this coke iron was supplied by the Horsehay Ironworks in Shropshire. From this date the percentage of coke iron used at these three forges was steadily increased. Coke iron was not introduced at the two Mitton forges until 1762-1763 and from then coke iron was only used intermittently. The Mitton forges were advantageously positioned near the navigable River Severn and were well situated for the import of pig iron from other regions of Britain. It was at these forges that the higher quality wrought iron was produced using imported tough iron. By 1765-66 Wolverley was using 90% coke iron to make wrought iron and this reached 100% in 1776-77. Cookley was using 90% coke iron in 1766-67 and this reached 100% in 1770-71. In 1779-80 the Knights' Stour forges used just over 1,300 tons of coke iron to help make wrought iron.

We will now examine the introduction of coke iron at the Knights' Stour forges in detail. The technology used for making wrought iron at the Stour forges was exactly the same as that used at the Coalbrookdale Forge during the period 1732-1738. A direct comparison can be made because coal was used in the chafery fires at the Knights' forges and also at the Coalbrookdale Forge. During the period 1744-1754 when only charcoal iron was used at Wolverley Forge, it took 1.40 loads of charcoal to make 1 ton of wrought iron. This is a very small overestimate as in some years small amounts of wrought iron were made using broken castings and scrap. Making iron from 'broken iron' consumed more fuel. The charcoal consumption figures for 1758-1780 have been slightly adjusted to compensate for the small amounts of wrought iron made from castings. I have attempted in Table One, using the charcoal consumption figures for Wolverley Forge (1758-1780), to project the result if 100%

coke iron was used in the finery. This gives us an average increase per ton of wrought iron made using coke iron of .21 load of charcoal. This answers well when compared with the results of those years when 100% of coke iron was used at the finery at Wolverley. This gives us an increase figure of .25 load of charcoal. Even more surprising is the very low increase in the amount of pig iron needed to convert into wrought iron when coke iron was used. The average for the period 1758-1780 when projected to 100% coke iron use at Wolverley gives us as low an increase as .005 ton of pig iron when making 1 ton of wrought iron (Table Two). The years 1758-1780 have been examined in detail because from 1758 an accurate record of how much coke iron used at the forges was kept. Before 1758 it is not certain how much of the coke iron was used and how much was remaindered to stock. After 1758 this record of coke iron use facilitated the calculations made by the forgemaster for extra labour costs in using coke iron. These extra labour costs worked out as £.075 per ton of coke iron fined. One advantage that coke iron seems to have given the forge operators is indicated by the run of several years of 100% coke iron use, so demonstrating that ordinary bar could be made without blending with any charcoal iron. The extra costs in using coke iron at the Wolverley Forge during L.1755-L.1756 is calculated as £0.57 per ton of wrought iron made. As well as extra costs in adopting coke iron so indeed there were savings. The Midlands area was a net importer of pig iron and during the period 1726-1801 the Knight family's forges bought pig iron from around 40 different charcoal furnaces. The use of a fairly local coke iron supply meant large savings on transport costs. In the period 1751-1754 the average freight and transport costs amounted to £0.38 per ton of wrought iron produced at Wolverley. During the time of 100% coke iron use at Wolverley the transport costs had dropped to £0.12 per ton of wrought iron made, a saving of £0.26 per ton. So the total increase of cost in using coke iron at Wolverley Forge in 1755-56 probably amounted to about £0.31 per ton of wrought iron produced. But could the use of coke iron have increased the fuel costs at the chafery? In around 1704 an ironmaster recorded that one load of coal could be used to draw out 2 tons of iron at the chafery.[17] This, indeed, is the ratio to be found at Wolverley before the introduction of coke iron. Calculations are made a little more difficult because the Stour accounts record the amount of coal used in loads (dozens), horse loads and tons. However, at Wolverley, in the late 1760s wagon loads were still used to record the amount of coal bought. In L.1768-L.1769 when 94.15% of the iron used at the forge was coke iron the ratio was still around a load of coal to 2 tons of iron at the chafery.

The figures for Cookley Forge give a similar result. In the period 1744-1754 the forge was using 1.43 loads of charcoal to make a ton of wrought iron. This can be compared with the projected 100% coke iron figures for 1758-1780 which gives us an increase of .29 load of charcoal per ton of wrought iron produced. The true 100% coke iron figures give an average increase of .23 load of charcoal (Table Four). The projected figures for Cookley give for 1758-1780 an increase of .03 ton of pig iron for making a ton of wrought iron using coke iron (Table Five). This gives an increase of costs in L.1755-L.1756 if 100% coke iron was used of £0.91. The transport cost saving in using coke iron would have been £0.35. This gives a total extra cost per ton of wrought iron produced from coke pig of £0.56. The figures for Whittington give a similar result. However, Whittington never reached 100% coke iron use as it was closed in 1771. The figures give us a charcoal consumption rate during the period 1744-1754 of 1.43 loads of charcoal to make a ton of wrought iron. The projected figures for 1758-1771 give an increase of .35 load of charcoal per ton of wrought iron made from coke iron. The pig iron/wrought iron ratio increases by .03 ton of pig iron per ton of wrought iron made. For the year L.1755-L.1756 this gives a cost increase of £1.02 per ton of wrought iron made using coke iron. However, Whittington was different to the two other forges because there were hardly any savings in transport costs through using coke iron. The coke iron reached the Stour from Shropshire via the River Severn. Whittington was the partnership's forge which was furthest away from the Severn. Whittington was also closely tied to Hales furnace and it experienced higher transport costs with Hales charcoal pig being brought across country. For these reasons Whittington Forge was closed down in 1771 and converted into a slitting mill. The conversion of coke iron into wrought iron was thereafter concentrated at Cookley and Wolverley.

The figures clearly demonstrate that the results from the three Stour forges hardly approach the fuel and iron consumptions experienced by the finers at Coalbrookdale in the period 1732-1738 (Table Seven). The conclusion is obvious which is that the coke iron used from 1754 at the Stour forges had completely different characteristics from the coke iron used at the Coalbrookdale Forge in the 1730s. There must have been a technical advance at the Coalbrookdale Ironworks in the early 1750s which helped to make a coke iron which was far easier to convert into wrought iron. Abiah Darby dated this innovation to 1753 and this could well be an accurate recollection. We must remember that Quakers, including Abiah Darby, kept journals, of mainly religious events, which could be used to tie back a specific event to a date.[18] The date of 1753 for this innovation stands well next to the Stour dates of 1754-55 for the adoption of coke iron at the Knight's forges.

Other evidence also points to the 'quality of iron' theory being the more likely candidate for the slowness of the industry in adopting the making of coke iron. The first use of coke iron at Wolverley Forge was when 6 tons were purchased from an independent dealer and not directly from the Coalbrookdale Ironworks. Were the Knights trying to set up an independent test of Coalbrookdale coke pigs at their forge? After the initial purchase all Coalbrookdale, Ketley and Horsehay coke iron was bought directly from the works. Other Shropshire ironworks also supplied coke pig iron to the Knights' forges, particularly the Lightmoor and Willey Ironworks. Coke iron from the Lightmoor Ironworks (George Perry & Co.) and the New Willey Ironworks (John Wilkinson & Co.) was introduced at only Wolverley in 1758-59. But only 1 ton of each was bought in that year, then larger quantities were purchased in the following years. This seems to point to the fact that both iron types were tested in 1758-59 to see if their quality matched up to the Darby product. Surely if it was a drop in price of coke iron which prompted its use in forges there would have been no need in testing the iron, and larger quantities would have been bought as a matter of course.

Another important change which affected the wrought iron industry was the successful use of coal as a fuel to convert pig iron into wrought iron. The first successful method of making wrought iron with coal was devised by the Wood family in the 1760s and became known as stamping and potting. The other more successful method was pioneered by Henry Cort in the 1780s and was known as the puddling process.[19] Both methods used coal as the fuel which was far cheaper than charcoal and so both methods saved money compared with the old finery and chafery method.

The economic pressures from the introduction of these new methods were soon felt at the old forges. The new cheap wrought iron produced a boost to the industry and extra sales soon prompted the spread of the new methods. The Knight family tried to answer this competition by commencing to manufacture the higher grade merchant bar at the Cookley site. However it was to be John Knight Jnr. who responded to the new technology by modernising and radically reorganising the Stour forges. This move was made in an effort to combat the competition from the integrated ironworks being founded in new iron making districts such as South Wales. This reorganisation dates from Ladyday 1796 when John Knight drew up a document detailing the state of his Stour forges and mills.[20] This document gives a detailed picture of the operation of the Stour works before modernisation. The two Mitton forges, which had at one time concentrated on making higher quality wrought iron, were then blooming forges making 9 tons of ordinary bars each week. Wolverley Forge was at this time standing idle having worked up all its stock, and Cookley Forge was making 6 tons of merchant bar per week. It was assessed that the Mitton forges each could produce a yearly total of 476 tons of wrought iron and Cookley could produce 312 tons of wrought iron in a year. In 1796 Whittington Mill was slitting iron from the Knight forges at a rate of 952 tons per year with a little spare capacity for slitting to hire at £0.80 a ton. Wolverley Mill which had been acquired recently was slitting to hire at £0.80 per ton but was not half supplied with bars.

Faced with this situation and increased competition, John Knight decided to modernise the forges and concentrate on producing higher quality wrought iron. He planned to have Mitton Lower as a blooming forge making 12 tons of best best bars each week. Wolverley would also be a blooming forge making 8 tons of best best bars each week and Cookley would make 8 tons of merchant bars each week. The radical change was to be made at Mitton Upper Forge which would become a balling forge making 20 tons of best bars weekly. To achieve this target it was necessary for Mitton Upper Forge to change over to the stamping and potting method of producing wrought iron. To this end a sum of £135 was spent at Mitton Upper Forge where an air furnace was built. A further £5 was spent on building a new hollow fire at Wolverley and £120 was expended on new machinery at Wolverley Mill. When the alterations were completed the new refining method was introduced.

The stamping and potting method of making wrought iron was developed by the Wood family in the 1750s and this work resulted in two patents being granted in 1761 and 1763. The name stamping and potting describes two of the stages of making wrought iron using this method. After a first melting of pig iron it was pounded under water to form small grains and then refined in a closed clay vessel or pot in a coal fired air furnace. The use of coal as the fuel in stamping and potting considerably reduced the costs in refining pig iron to wrought iron. In 1796 John Knight calculated that the fuel cost for making one ton of best bars at Mitton Upper Forge with stamping and potting would be £2.12. Calculations were also made for fuel costs for producing a ton of best best bars at Mitton Lower Forge with the old finery and chafery method. Although the wrought iron was of a slightly higher grade the fuel costs do indicate the savings that could be made using stamping and potting. The fuel costs for making a ton of wrought iron using the old method at Mitton Lower Forge was as high as £3.83. There was one disadvantage with stamping and potting and that was an increase in the consumption of pig iron. Knight calculated that with stamping and potting at Mitton Upper Forge it would take 1.65 tons of pig iron to make a ton of best bar. He also calculated that at Mitton Lower Forge which used the finery and chafery method it would take 1.33 tons of pig iron to make a ton of best best bars. However, this extra consumption of pig iron was defrayed cost wise by fuel savings and the fact that the stamping and potting method could use 100% grey coke iron while the finery and chafery method necessitated the use of a proportion of expensive tough iron.

John Knight's forge plans were put into operation during L.1796-97 when Mitton Upper Forge began stamping and potting. However, the process used was probably Wright and Jesson's refinement of the original method. The pig iron would first be heated in a normal refinery using coke. The product was then taken out as lumps and beaten into plates under a large flat stamp. The plates were then broken under a round stamp into small pieces. The pieces were then cleansed of the 'sulphurous matter' by washing in a rolling barrel. The washed residues were then heated in a common air furnace in pots or otherwise with coals or coke and then shaped in a chafery. Wright and Jesson's first patent for these methods was granted on the 2nd December 1773. A later patent was granted to Wright and Jesson on the 6th March for a further refinement to their method. The modification to the original method was that cakes or plates of iron were piled on top of each other and heated in a coal fired reverberatory furnace. This replaced the heating of the iron in pots. Wright and Jesson's method (piling) certainly seems to have found favour with the forge owners of the English Midlands.[21] However, there is evidence in the accounts of the Stour Partnership that both potting and piling were carried out at the Knight forges. The presence of reverberatory furnaces and the use of the piling method are indicated by the fact that stamped and puddled iron were later produced at one forge using the same furnaces and equipment. The Knights seem to have slightly adapted the stamping and potting method for use in their forges. The 1796 estimates for Mitton Upper Forge and the later accounts show that a small amount of charcoal was used as a fuel with this method. This seems to mirror a refinement of making wrought iron with coal pioneered at the Carron Ironworks in Scotland. This technique was described in the following terms by one of the partners in the Carron venture,

> *.... of the various methods of converting pigs into bar iron lately tried at Carron, that of bringing it to nature with Pit Coal, afterwards sinking it*

*with charcoal and drawing it in the Hollow Fire has hitherto succeeded best as to cheapness.*[22]

It is interesting to note that members of the Knight family had visited Edinburgh to attend chemistry lectures and while there visited ironworks in the area.

The adoption of stamping set about a series of changes at the Stour forges that at times prove difficult to follow. Mitton Upper Forge began to use the stamping process in L.1796-97 and so successful was its adoption that Mitton Lower Forge converted to the new method in the following year. Mitton Lower Forge also began to refine pig iron. The refinery used for this purpose was a small rectangular hearth which was coke fired. The temperature within the refinery was raised with an air blast. The pig iron melted in the hearth where a slag formed on top containing silicon, phosphorus and sulphur. The slag and molten iron were separated and the final product was a higher quality iron than that charged at the beginning of the process. Refining iron often increased the quality of the pig iron from grey to white. This refined iron was then used instead of tough iron in the old finery process to make wrought iron. The use of refining allowed the Knights to reduce their purchases of the expensive charcoal tough iron. The cheaper coke iron could now be refined to replace this expensive iron. In L.1798-99 Mitton Upper Forge also began to refine pigs for the other charcoal forges. Another important change took place in L.1799-1800 when the two Mitton forges began puddling alongside the stamping method. Mitton Upper Forge then ceased stamping but both methods continued at the lower forge.

Puddling was carried out in a reverberatory furnace where molten iron and burning coal were kept separate. When the pig iron had become molten it was stirred using iron bars. Eventually bubbling took place and blue carbon monoxide flames were given off. After prolonged stirring the iron became spongy and was formed into a large ball of iron. It was then removed from the furnace and taken to a forge hammer where slag particles were squeezed out and the metal shaped. The final operation was to pass the iron at welding heat through a set of grooved rolls. Puddling was cheaper than stamping and output with Cort's method was greater. So successful was puddling at the Knight forges that in L.1800-01 Wolverley also began to refine and puddle iron. In the following year Cookley was only employed in drawing and finishing wrought iron. Such was the increased output of wrought iron from puddling that it was decided to turn Wolverley completely over to heating and rolling blooms produced by the Mitton forges. This took place in L.1803-04 and during that year to keep this facility fully employed 311.75 tons of blooms were purchased from J. Bishton of the Snedshill Ironworks for rolling and finishing. When Wolverley stopped puddling the supply of blooms was decreased, and for two years Cookley Forge made some using stamping until the output of the Mitton forges increased. When this was achieved Cookley Forge returned to finishing or drawing iron only during L.1805-06. Wolverley in that year was rolling bars from the other forges and blooms from George Attwood (Dudley Wood Ironworks) and John Bishton. Mitton Upper Forge was at this time refining, puddling, rolling and drawing with Mitton Lower Forge refining, puddling and stamping. Bromford Forge had also been converted to stamping and then changed to puddling. In the final years of the partnership John Knight had completely changed the character of his family's Stour forges. They were no longer independent producers of wrought iron but were inter-dependent components within a larger organisation. By the end of the partnership Mitton Upper Forge was refining, puddling and drawing, Mitton Lower was refining and stamping, Cookley was drawing iron, Whittington was slitting and rolling hoops and Wolverley was slitting and rolling. Bromford was now refining and puddling. There is also evidence in the accounts of the manufacture in the forges of puddler's stamped iron. This was made when puddled iron was shingled into slabs and then broken up, piled, reheated and hammered into blooms or billets. The blooms could then be reheated and rolled into bars or other forms. These developments can be viewed as a bewildering set of changes with a change at one forge initiating changes at the other sites. The fact that different stages in the operation of producing wrought iron were tackled by different forges, added to the periodic buying in of blooms for finishing, makes assessing output a difficult task. However, a considerable increase in output of wrought iron is hinted at by the sales figures. In the previous year to the modernisation of the forges sales of iron reached 2,174.55 tons but during L.1807-08 sales of iron from the Stour Partnership were recorded as 4,020.6 tons.

Within twelve years John Knight had reorganised the forges of the Stour Partnership and changed them from the old type charcoal method to new processes using coke and coal as the fuels. This was not to be the end of the modernisation of the forges even though the Stour Partnership was dissolved in 1810. These changes were to continue for those sites which were to be the properties owned by John Knight & Co.

**References.**


1. The best accounts of the finery and chafery method can be found in H.R.Schubert, *History of the British Iron and Steel Industry from c.450 B.C. to A.D. 1775*, 1957, pp. 272-291. Alex den Ouden, The Production of Wrought Iron in Finery Hearths, Part One, *Journal of the Historical Metallurgy Society*, Vol. 15, 1981, No. 2, pp.63-87.
2. This chapter is based upon information gleaned from the accounts of the Bringewood Partnership and Stour Partnership, Kidderminster Public Library. Knight Manuscripts.
3. K.P.L.,K.M., 243, Weekly Forge Accounts, July 2nd 1763-April 19th 1766.
4. B.R.L., B.& W., List of Ironworks, 1794.
5. H.R.O., D.C.P., Bundle 407, Particulars of what was in Bringewood Forge and Charlcotte Furnace at the time Mr. Edward Knight died, June 11th 1783.
6. K.P.L.,K.P., 6758, Original Calculations Regarding the Ironworks, Ladyday 1796.
7. Marie B. Rowlands, *Masters and Men in the Metalware Trades before the Industrial Revolution*, Manchester, 1975, pp. 63-66.

8. R.A.Lewis, *Two Partnerships of the Knights - A Study of the Midland Iron Industry in the Eighteenth Century*, M.A. Thesis, Birmingham University, 1949, p.22.
9. C.K.Hyde, The Iron Industry in the West Midlands in 1754 : Observations from the Travel Diary of Charles Wood, *West Midlands Studies*, Vol. 6, 1973, pp. 39-40.
10. Barrie Trinder, *The Industrial Revolution in Shropshire*, Chichester, 1973, p. 30.
11. C.K.Hyde, *Technological Change and the British Iron Industry*, Princeton, 1973.
12. C.K.Hyde, *Technological Change*, p. 38.
13. C.K.Hyde, *Technological Change*, pp. 38-40.
14. J.R.Harris, *The British Iron Industry 1700-1850*, 1988, pp. 36-37.
15. C.K.Hyde, *Technological Change*, p. 38.
16. C.K.Hyde, *Technological Change*, p.28.
17. H.R.Schubert, op. cit., p. 426.
18. Rachel Labouchere, *Abiah Darby*, York, 1988, pp. 57-64.
19. For both processes see, R.A.Mott (Ed. P.Singer), *Henry Cort: The Great Finer*, 1983, pp. 2-8 & 37-39.
20. K.P.L., K.M., 6758, Original Calculations Regarding the Ironworks, Ladyday 1796.
21. R.A.Mott (Ed. P.Singer), op. cit., pp. 12-13.
22. R.H.Campbell, *Carron Company*, Edinburgh, 1961, p. 58.

## Table One: Charcoal Consumption at Wolverley Forge.

1744-54 gives figures of 1 ton wrought iron made to 1.4 loads of charcoal used.

| Year | Output of wrought iron & percentage coke iron used. (tons) | Charcoal total* (loads) | Charcoal used per ton of wrought iron made | Increase/ decrease | Projected increase with 100% coke iron |
|---|---|---|---|---|---|
| 1758-59 | 302 (32.45%) | 418.55 | 1.38 | -.02 | 0 |
| 1759-60 | 300.75 (51.27%) | 424.85 | 1.41 | +.01 | .02 |
| 1760-61 | 289 (45.55%) | 415.25 | 1.44 | +.04 | .09 |
| 1761-62 | 268.5 (38.46%) | 376.72 | 1.4 | 0 | 0 |
| 1762-63 | 272 (44.7%) | 390.25 | 1.43 | +.03 | .07 |
| 1763-64 | 270.5 (48.07%) | 393.47 | 1.45 | +.05 | .10 |
| 1764-65 | 287 (66.47%) | 432.25 | 1.51 | +.11 | .16 |
| 1765-66 | 223.5 (90%) | 346.72 | 1.55 | +.15 | .17 |
| 1766-67 | 274.5 (95.05%) | 454.5 | 1.65 | +.25 | .26 |
| 1767-68 | 278 (99.22%) | 427.67 | 1.54 | +.14 | .14 |
| 1768-69 | 259.5 (94.15%) | 408.25 | 1.57 | +.17 | .18 |
| 1769-70 | 256.5 (99.41%) | 422.45 | 1.65 | +.25 | .25 |
| 1770-71 | 272.5 (97.2%) | 480.37 | 1.76 | +.36 | .37 |
| 1771-72 | 290.5 (94.55%) | 471.32 | 1.62 | +.22 | .23 |
| 1772-73 | 299.25 (77.84%) | 551.27 | 1.84 | +.44 | .56 |
| 1773-74 | 290.5 (78.23%) | 530 | 1.82 | +.42 | .54 |
| 1774-75 | 306.5 (80.91%) | 488.82 | 1.59 | +.19 | .23 |
| 1775-76 | 316 (98.86%) | 516.6 | 1.63 | +.23 | .23 |
| 1776-77 | 309.5 (100%) | 529.67 | 1.71 | +.31 | .31 |
| 1777-78 | 295.5 (100%) | 498.27 | 1.69 | +.29 | .29 |
| 1778-79 | 347 (100%) | 565.47 | 1.63 | +.23 | .23 |
| 1779-80 | 344 (100%) | 536.12 | 1.56 | +.16 | .16 |

Overall average increase in using coke iron = .21 load of charcoal for each ton of wrought iron made.

Average increase in using coke iron taken from 100% figures = .25 load of charcoal for each ton of wrought iron made.

* - These figures have been slightly adjusted because in some years wrought iron was made from broken castings etc. The making of wrought iron from castings used up more fuel than when using pigs. These are only small amounts so the figure of 1.4 loads of charcoal for 1744-54 is a slight over estimate for fuel consumption. Take 1771-72 for instance, in that year 290.5 tons of wrought iron were made from pigs and 12 tons were made from castings. I have taken 12 x 1.4 loads of charcoal from the total fuel consumption. 1.4 loads of charcoal is an under estimate of the fuel required to make a ton of wrought iron from castings, this should be balanced by the earlier over estimate. The wrought iron made from castings do not appear in the table.

*Plate Four* *Trimming an ancony in the chafery part of a forge (Diderot's Encyclopedie)*

# Table Two: Pig iron/Wrought iron conversion rates at Wolverley Forge.

1744-54 gives figures of 1 ton of wrought iron made from 1.33 tons of pig iron.

| Year | Output of wrought iron & percentage coke iron used. (tons) | Amount of pig iron used to produce 1 ton of wrought iron. | Increase/ decrease | Projected increase with 100% coke iron. (tons) |
|---|---|---|---|---|
| 1758-59 | 302 (32.45%) | 1.28 | -.05 | 0 |
| 1759-60 | 300.75 (51.27%) | 1.26 | -.07 | 0 |
| 1760-61 | 289 (45.55%) | 1.25 | -.08 | 0 |
| 1761-62 | 268.5 (38.46%) | 1.26 | -.07 | 0 |
| 1762-63 | 272 (44.7%) | 1.28 | -.05 | 0 |
| 1763-64 | 270.5 (48.07%) | 1.25 | -.08 | 0 |
| 1764-65 | 287 (66.47%) | 1.25 | -.08 | 0 |
| 1765-66 | 223.5 (90%) | 1.28 | -.05 | 0 |
| 1766-67 | 274.5 (95.05%) | 1.28 | -.05 | 0 |
| 1767-68 | 278 (99.22%) | 1.32 | -.01 | 0 |
| 1768-69 | 259.5 (94.15%) | 1.28 | -.05 | 0 |
| 1769-70 | 256.5 (99.41%) | 1.28 | -.05 | 0 |
| 1770-71 | 272.5 (97.2%) | 1.30 | -.03 | 0 |
| 1771-72 | 290.5 (94.55%) | 1.27 | -.06 | 0 |
| 1772-73 | 299.25 (77.84%) | 1.32 | -.01 | 0 |
| 1773-74 | 290.5 (78.23%) | 1.38 | +.05 | .06 |
| 1774-75 | 306.5 (80.91%) | 1.35 | +.02 | .02 |
| 1775-76 | 316 (98.86%) | 1.32 | -.01 | 0 |
| 1776-77 | 309.5 (100%) | 1.34 | +.01 | .01 |
| 1777-78 | 295.5 (100%) | 1.33 | 0 | 0 |
| 1778-79 | 347 (100%) | 1.34 | +.01 | .01 |
| 1779-80 | 344 (100%) | 1.35 | +.02 | .02 |

Overall average increase in using coke iron = .005 ton of iron in making 1 ton of wrought iron.

Table Three: The increase in Costs of using Coke Iron at Wolverley Forge in the Year Ladyday 1755 to Ladyday 1756.

| | **per ton of wrought iron made** |
|---|---|
| Extra charcoal cost (.21 load) | £0.44 |
| Extra cost of coke iron (.005 ton) | £0.03 |
| Extra labour costs (£0.075 per ton used) | £0.10 |
| TOTAL | £0.57 |
| Transport & Freight Savings. | |
| 1751-52 costs per ton wrought iron made | £0.49 |
| 1752-53 costs per ton wrought iron made | £0.30 |
| 1753-54 costs per ton wrought iron made | £0.34 |
| Average costs | £0.38 |
| 1776-77 costs per ton wrought iron made | £0.13 |
| 1777-78 costs per ton wrought iron made | £0.10 |
| 1778-79 costs per ton wrought iron made | £0.14 |
| Average costs | £0.12 |

A saving of £0.26 per ton made.
Total extra costs per ton made = £0.57 - £0.26 = £0.31

# Table Four: Charcoal Consumption at Cookley Forge.

1744-54 gives figures of 1 ton of wrought iron made to 1.43 loads of charcoal used

| Year | Output of wrought iron & percentage coke iron used. (tons) | Charcoal total (loads) | Charcoal used per ton of wrought iron (loads) | Increase/ decrease | Projected increase with 100% coke iron |
|---|---|---|---|---|---|
| 1758-59 | 248 (32%) | 388.84 | 1.57 | +.14 | .43 |
| 1759-60 | 260.5 (45.7%) | 420.22 | 1.61 | +.18 | .39 |
| 1760-61 | 295 (46.58%) | 466.25 | 1.58 | +.15 | .32 |
| 1761-62 | 288 (46.54%) | 449.13 | 1.56 | +.13 | .28 |
| 1762-63 | 257.5 (50.68%) | 418.25 | 1.62 | +.19 | .37 |
| 1763-64 | 220 (42.42%) | 347.88 | 1.58 | +.15 | .35 |
| 1764-65 | 291.5 (68.99%) | 471 | 1.62 | +.19 | .27 |
| 1765-66 | 252.17 (82.42%) | 414.56 | 1.64 | +.21 | .25 |
| 1766-67 | 257.5 (93.46%) | 450.71 | 1.75 | +.32 | .34 |
| 1767-68 | 256 (75.5%) | 393.28 | 1.54 | +.11 | .15 |
| 1768-69 | 276.5 (84.59%) | 441.62 | 1.60 | +.17 | .20 |
| 1769-70 | 260 (95.43%) | 445.29 | 1.71 | +.28 | .29 |
| 1770-71 | 251.25 (100%) | 431.62 | 1.72 | +.29 | .29 |
| 1771-72 | 286.5 (99%) | 454.16 | 1.58 | +.15 | .15 |
| 1772-73 | 306 (91.96%) | 516.09 | 1.69 | +.26 | .28 |
| 1773-74 | 287 (80.41%) | 519.75 | 1.81 | +.38 | .47 |
| 1774-75 | 292.5 (77.36%) | 491.17 | 1.68 | +.25 | .32 |
| 1775-76 | 314 (100%) | 529.93 | 1.69 | +.26 | .26 |
| 1776-77 | 318 (100%) | 497 | 1.56 | +.13 | .13 |
| 1777-78 | 301.5 (99.75%) | 530.58 | 1.76 | +.33 | .33 |
| 1778-79 | 305 (100%) | 506.37 | 1.66 | +.23 | .23 |
| 1779-80 | 304.5 (100%) | 502.27 | 1.65 | +.22 | .22 |

Overall average increase in using coke iron = .29 load of charcoal for each ton of wrought iron made,

Average increase in using coke iron taken from 100% figures = .23 load of charcoal for each ton of wrought iron made.

# Table Five: Pig Iron/Wrought Iron Conversion Rates at Cookley Forge.

1745-55 gives figures of 1 ton of wrought iron made from 1.33 tons of pig iron.

| Year | Output of wrought iron & percentage coke iron used. (tons) | Amount of pig iron used to produce 1 ton of wrought iron. (tons) | Increase/ decrease | Projected increase with 100% coke iron |
|---|---|---|---|---|
| 1758-59 | 248 (32%) | 1.37 | +.04 | .12 |
| 1759-60 | 260.5 (45.7%) | 1.39 | +.06 | .13 |
| 1760-61 | 295 (46.58%) | 1.35 | +.02 | .04 |
| 1761-62 | 288 (46.54%) | 1.40 | +.07 | .15 |
| 1762-63 | 257.5 (50.68%) | 1.39 | +.06 | .12 |
| 1763-64 | 220 (42.42%) | 1.34 | +.01 | .02 |
| 1764-65 | 291.5 (68.99%) | 1.34 | +.01 | .01 |
| 1765-66 | 252.17 (82.42%) | 1.34 | +.01 | .01 |
| 1766-67 | 257.5 (93.46%) | 1.34 | +.01 | .01 |
| 1767-68 | 256 (75.5%) | 1.37 | +.04 | .05 |
| 1768-69 | 276.5 (84.59%) | 1.34 | +.01 | .01 |
| 1769-70 | 260 (95.43%) | 1.34 | +.01 | .01 |
| 1770-71 | 251.25 (100%) | 1.33 | 0 | 0 |
| 1771-72 | 286.5 (99%) | 1.30 | -.03 | 0 |
| 1772-73 | 306 (91.96%) | 1.34 | +.01 | .01 |
| 1773-74 | 287 (80.41%) | 1.34 | +.01 | .01 |
| 1774-75 | 292.5 (77.36%) | 1.32 | -.01 | 0 |
| 1775-76 | 314 (100%) | 1.33 | 0 | 0 |
| 1776-77 | 318 (100%) | 1.34 | +.01 | .01 |
| 1777-78 | 301.5 (99.75%) | 1.36 | +.03 | .03 |
| 1778-79 | 305 (100%) | 1.37 | +.04 | .04 |
| 1779-80 | 304.5 (100%) | 1.33 | 0 | 0 |

Overall increase in using coke iron = .03 ton of iron in making 1 ton of wrought iron.

## Table Six: The Increase in Costs of Using Coke Iron at Cookley Forge in the Year Ladyday 1755 to Ladyday 1756.

| | **per ton of wrought iron made** |
|---|---|
| Extra charcoal cost (.29 load) | £0.61 |
| Extra cost of coke iron (.03 ton) | £0.20 |
| Extra labour costs (.075 per ton used) | £0.10 |
| TOTAL | £0.91 |
| Transport & Freight Savings. | |
| 1751-52 costs per ton of wrought iron made | £0.52 |
| 1752-53 costs per ton of wrought iron made | £0.66 |
| 1753-54 costs per ton of wrought iron made | £0.37 |
| Average costs | £0.52 |
| 1776-77 costs per ton of wrought iron made | £0.15 |
| 1777-78 costs per ton of wrought iron made | £0.15 |
| 1778-79 costs per ton of wrought iron made | £0.22 |
| Average costs | £0.17 |

A saving of £0.35 per ton made.
Total extra costs per ton made = £0.91 - £0.35 = £0.56

## Table Seven: Input Data for Coalbrookdale and the Stour Forges.

| | **Coalbrookdale 1732-38** | **Wolverley 1758-80** | **Cookley 1758-80** | **Whittington 1758-71** |
|---|---|---|---|---|
| Charcoal used in making a ton of wrought iron with coke pig iron | 3.06 | 1.61 | 1.72 | 1.78 loads |
| Coke pig iron used | 1.41 | 1.335 | 1.36 | 1.36 tons |

*Plate Five* *An eighteenth century slitting mill (Diderot's Encyclopedie)*

Figure Four - The Mitton Forges.

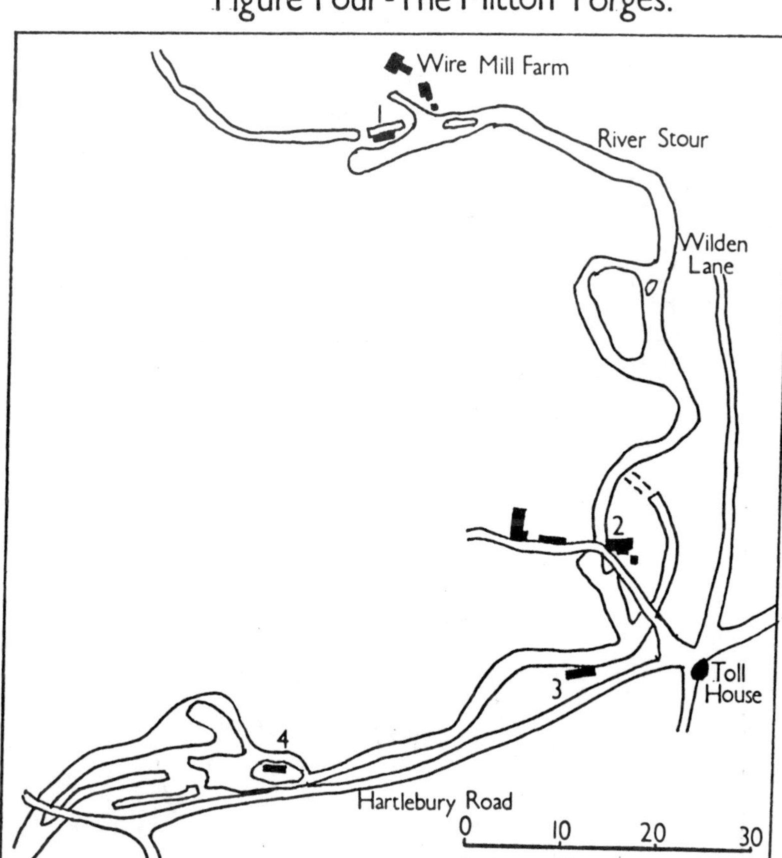


KEY

1 - Mitton Upper Forge Finery

2 - Mitton Upper Forge Chafery (Jenny Hole, later a corn mill)

3 - Mitton Lower Forge Finery

4 - Mitton Lower Forge Chafery (Hammersmith Forge)

Map partly based on 1834 tithe map

Figure Five - Bar Iron Prices at the Stour Forges 1727-1736.

| Year | Best bars | Ordinary bars | Blended bars | Coldshort bars |
|---|---|---|---|---|
| L.1727-28 | £19.70 | £18.70 | - | - |
| 1728-29 | £17.50 | £17.00 | - | - |
| 1729-30 | - | - | - | - |
| 1730-31 | £17.25 | £16.74 | £16.25 | £13.98 |
| 1731-32 | £17.21 | £16.76 | £16.36 | £15.74 |
| 1732-33 | £17.00 | £15.50 | £15.14 | £14.42 |
| 1733-34 | £16.02 | £14.50 | - | - |
| 1734-35 | £16.00 | £14.25 | £13.72 | £13.30 |
| 1735-36 | £15.50 | £14.00 | £13.56 | £13.07 |

Figure Six - The Cost of a Load of Charcoal Consumed at Wolverley Forge.

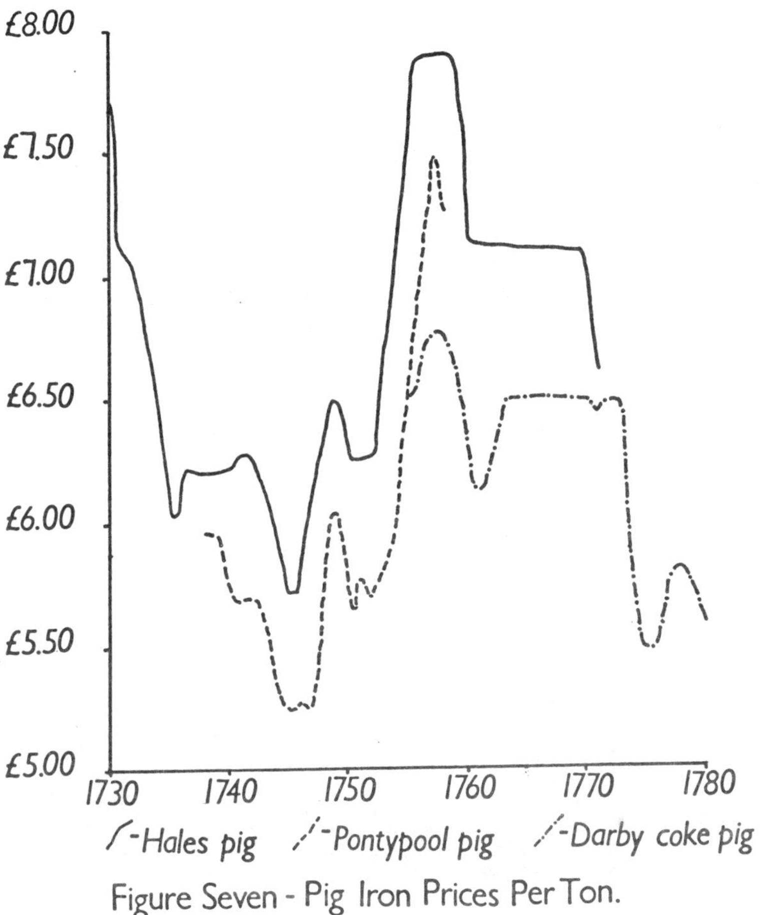


Figure Seven - Pig Iron Prices Per Ton.

*Plate Six* *Frederic Winn Knight (1812-1897)*

# Chapter Six.

## John Knight & Co., 1810-1850.

When the old Knight partnership was dissolved some of the assets were sold, some were transferred to Isaac Spooner and some remained in the hands of John Knight. He formed John Knight & Co. to operate the remaining works in the Stour Valley. These properties consisted of Cookley Forge, Mitton Upper Forge and Wolverley Lower Mill. The company consisted of John Knight who held a ¾ share and William Hancocks who possessed a ¼ share.[1] This partnership now had to formulate a new strategy for iron production at their works. John Knight knew only too well the sort of competition he was facing from the new integrated ironworks founded in areas such as South Wales. John Knight was aware of the situation in South Wales from personal experience as he had been a leading light in forming the Varteg Hill Iron Company which built and operated a coke furnace at Varteg near Blaenavon from 1803.[2] He had probably been attracted to invest in this area because of the presence of Thomas Hill, a Stourport banker, in the Blaenavon Iron Company. The Knight forges had been purchasing Blaenavon pig iron for conversion from 1791. Purchases of pig iron from the Varteg Hill Iron Company commenced in 1803 and fairly soon after this refined metal was also being bought from Varteg. It was a bold decision that John Knight made to withdraw from the Varteg Hill Company and to invest his capital in the Stour forges in what was a rather ancient iron making area. The withdrawal of John Knight from his South Wales investment probably took place when John Knight & Co. took over the Stour works of the old Knight partnership.

The sale of Varteg provided the company with money to invest in their Stour properties. John Knight had lost none of the drive and innovative thinking that he had shown during the earlier modernisation of the Stour forges. A steam engine was now purchased to drive rolling mills at Cookley where wrought iron was being made using two different methods. The making of wrought iron using charcoal as a fuel ceased, and wrought iron bars and bolts began to be produced by the mills at Cookley. Wolverley Lower Mill continued to roll and slit wrought iron but a new product began to be manufactured at this site. This was the making of wire and in L.1810-11 output began at 7,472 bundles. Mitton Upper Forge continued to refine pig iron, make wrought iron and also roll and slit iron. A profit of £2,547.8 was made by John Knight & Co. in its first year of operation which was followed in the next year by a loss of £327.75. Profits were restored to the company in L.1812-13 and the partnership remained profitable during the next thirty seven years.

The manufacture of wire proved so profitable that this trade was introduced at Mitton Upper Forge, and in L.1814-15 Wolverley Lower Mill manufactured 10,028 bundles of wire with Mitton Upper Forge producing 215¼ bundles. In the same year

Cookley was producing wrought iron with some refining also taking place. Finished products issuing from the Cookley site included rods, rolled bars and sheet iron. John Knight & Co., with its varied products, seems to have weathered well the widespread depression in the British iron industry that took place at the end of the Napoleonic Wars. However, the wrought iron produced at the forges must have received stiff competition from the same product being manufactured by works situated on coalfields. Cookley was some distance away from coal reserves and so this increased the fuel costs in making wrought iron even though Cookley and Wolverley were situated next to the Staffordshire and Worcestershire Canal. Cookley was not surrounded by reserves of coal but was surrounded by another raw material which was now being under used. This was wood and charcoal. Wrought iron made with charcoal was still considered to be the best material for the manufacture of the highest quality tinplate. John Knight & Co. therefore made a brave decision to return to the manufacture of charcoal wrought iron and to produce tinplate with this product. This was to take place at the Cookley site where there was room for expansion between the canal and the River Stour. So the Knight family returned to making a product that they had pioneered when tinplate was manufactured at Bringewood and Mitton Lower Forge during the period 1740-1775. Purchases of charcoal were made, and in L.1814-15 tinning commenced with the company producing 1,386 boxes of tinplate during the year.

More and more of the partnership's manufacturing operations were now taking place at the Cookley Ironworks, and it is not surprising that production at Mitton Upper Forge was abandoned in L.1816-17. The Wolverley Wire Mills remained in operation and being approximately 1¼ miles away from Cookley could be easily administered from the main works. Mitton Upper Forge was roughly 5¼ miles away from Cookley and communication between the three works must have been difficult.

It is an illustration of the changing nature of the iron industry that the company decided to convert Mitton Upper Forge into a corn mill in an attempt to rent it out. The Knights for some time held two forges at Mitton. These were called Mitton Upper Forge and Mitton Lower Forge. Unfortunately later historians corrupted the names to Upper Mitton Forge and Lower Mitton Forge. In fact both forges were closer to Lower Mitton than Upper Mitton. Just to confuse matters further, both sites consisted of two parts, the upper and lower forges. Both Mitton forges had fineries with a downstream chafery, often called a hammerman's or hammersmith's forge. The lower part of Mitton Upper Forge was also called Jenny Hole Forge.[3] For the corn mill conversion it was necessary to take bricks, tiles and timber from the upper part to enlarge the lower part into a complete corn mill. Three dwelling houses at the site were also converted into a stable and it was hoped to lease the premises for £150 a year. There were a further eleven tenements with gardens and a large stable for rent which it was hoped would bring in an additional fifty to sixty pounds per year. The conversion of the forge to a corn mill cost just over £654 and it was immediately rented out at a yearly rate of £157.5.[4]

A glimpse of the large range of products made by John Knight & Co. is provided by the list of items in stock for L.1819-20. At Cookley there were gun lumps, wire lumps, puddler's stamped iron, charcoal stamped iron. puddler's bars best, puddler's bars common, wire billets, best billets, charcoal blooms, tin blooms, small rounds, osborn rods, nail rods, charcoal rods, best rods, spoon rods, hoops, strip iron and sheet iron. At the tin mill the stock included charcoal bars, blackplates, loose plates and finished plates while stock at the Wolverley Mill included osborn rods, common rods and finished wire. Tinplate stocks were also housed at the premises of merchants including Swan, Chappell & Co. of London and Acraman & Son of Bristol.

It is interesting to note that wrought iron at Cookley was produced using the charcoal method, by puddling and also with the continued method of refining in a reverberatory furnace with some stamping. Coke was used with this process and the product was called puddler's stamped iron but later came to be known as coke iron.

The continued profitability of John Knight & Co. can be ascribed to the fact that three differing products were produced, namely wire, wrought iron and tinplate. Quite often depressions in the iron industry and the tinplate trade did not necessarily coincide and this helped keep the company on an even keel. One major problem did occur in the year L.1828-29 when one of the main tinplate merchants that John Knight & Co. dealt with became insolvent. The failure of Swan, Chappell & Co. cost the company a loss of £5,000 with yearly profits dropping from £13,641 to £8,704. Profits recovered in L.1833-34 rising to £20,709.5 for L.1838-39. These high profits occurred during boom conditions in the iron trade, partly generated by a great expansion in railway building. This more than offset the problems experienced by the British tinplate industry following the American financial crisis of 1833-37. Exports of tinplate had grown from 2,500 tons in 1805 to 9,000 tons in 1837 with America being destined to be the greatest market for British tinplate.[5] Occasionally there are written in the company's accounts explanations qualifying the year's financial figures. In the accounts for L.1834-35 the following is added to the final balance sheet to explain the high profits made during the year,

> *We had no idea of this account turning out so well but it has been a good year's work and we have made many tinplates of puddled iron which were formerly made (at much greater expense) with cokes.*

In the next year's accounts can be found these comments,

> *Nearly £7000 of this year's large produce might be accounted for by the great advances upon iron and tinplates during the year and which we reap the benefit in this account by valuing our stock at the times' prices, when a reaction takes place this must be kept in view.*

From the mid 1820s onwards changes were taking place in the ownership of the company. This led to a reduction in John Knight's holding as can be discerned from the following company details;

L.1823-24. ---- John Knight (5⁄8), William Hancocks (1⁄4), John Hancocks (1⁄8).

L.1826-27. ---- John Knight (1⁄2), William Hancocks (1⁄4), John Hancocks (1⁄4).

L.1831-32. ---- John Knight (18⁄48), William Hancocks (10⁄48), John Hancocks (5⁄48), William Piper (5⁄48), John Brown (6⁄48), Samuel Hancocks (2⁄48), William Hancocks Jnr. (2⁄48).

L.1832-33. ---- John Knight (18⁄48), William Hancocks (10⁄48), John Hancocks (7⁄48), John Brown (6⁄48), Samuel Hancocks (3⁄48), William Hancocks Jnr. (4⁄48).

These changes in the partnership meant that on Ladyday 1832 John Knight lost overall control of the company to the Hancocks' family. John Knight's actions in reducing his interest in the company can be easily understood. In 1830 Knight had taken up residence at Simonsbath House on Exmoor where for some time he had been making purchases of land. His energies were now being channelled away from the iron trade to his scheme for farming part of Exmoor's wild lands.[6] However, in 1837 his wife's health began to fail and they moved to Trinity Manor House on the island of Jersey. Two years later the family moved to Rome where they lived in Palazzo Bracci, Via Rassella.[7]

John Knight now further reduced his own personal commitment to the company by introducing his sons into the partnership. On Ladyday 1842, Frederic Winn Knight took over three of his father's shares. Two years later the two other sons, Charles Allanson Knight and Edward Lewis Knight, entered the partnership when the shares were allocated in the following manner.

L.1844-45. ---- John Knight (11⁄48), Frederic Winn Knight (4⁄48), Charles Allanson Knight (3⁄48), Edward Lewis Knight (1⁄48), John Hancocks (12⁄48), Samuel Hancocks (4⁄48), William Hancocks Jnr. (9⁄48), with four shares being reserved for future allotment. These were purchased later by Matthew Heath on Ladyday 1846.

The death of John Knight took place in 1850 and this marked the end of an era for the company. It had been John Knight who had modernised and welded together the remaining properties of the old Stour Partnership into an economic manufacturer of wrought iron and tinplate. He had been the guiding hand in the business from 1796 when he drew up the document detailing his plans for modernising the old charcoal forges along the Stour.

The death of John Knight left the company owned by the following partners.

1850. --------- Executors of John Knight (11⁄48), Frederic Winn Knight (4⁄48), Charles Allanson Knight (3⁄48), Edward Lewis Knight (1⁄48), Executors of John Hancocks (14⁄48), William Hancocks Jnr. (9⁄48), Matthew Heath (6⁄48).

The business was at this time in a fairly good state with a profit of £12,635 being made during L.1849-50. Wire was still being made at Wolverley and a large range of products was emanating from Cookley. These included wrought iron bars, rods, sheet iron, castings and tinplate. Such was the standing of the name of the founder of the company that it was decided to continue the business under the style of John Knight & Co.

**References.**

1. All statements concerning partnerships, profits, products and outputs are extracted from, K.P.L., K.M., Accounts of John Knight & Co., 1810-1850. 200-239.
2. B.R.L., B.& W., List of Ironworks, 1806.

3. B.R.L., B.& W., The list of ironworks of 1794 calls the complete Upper Mitton Forge by the name of Ginnyhole.
4. K.P.L., K.M., 6480.
5. W.E.Minchinton, *The British Tinplate Industry - A History*, Oxford, 1957, pp. 27-28.
6. C.S.Orwin & R.J. Sellick, *The Reclamation of Exmoor* Forest, Newton Abbot, 1970.
7. C.S.Orwin & R.J.Sellick, op. cit., pp. 32-33.

# Chapter Seven.

## The Cookley and Brockmoor Works.

The 1850s saw changes at the company's ironworks sites and also in the financial organisation of the partnership. It was decided to concentrate all the manufacturing processes at the Cookley Iron and Tinplate Works and so the Wolverley Wire Mill was sold off between 1853 and 1859.[1] The new owners were Thomas Banks and Thomas Morgan who were described in the lease as iron and tinplate manufacturers of Kidderminster. The partnership was now divided into sixty shares each valued at £1,000. By 1869 the Cookley partnership consisted of Frederic Winn Knight (10 shares), Charles Allanson Knight (8), Edward Lewis Knight (2), William Hancocks Jnr. (11), Matthew Heath (10), John Saunders (10), Alfred John Hancocks (4) and Augustus Talbot Hancocks (5). However, this partnership was dissolved on the 26th of March 1869 and a new one set up consisting of Frederic Winn Knight (20 shares), Charles Allanson Knight (10), Edward Lewis Knight (5), Walter Raleigh Browne (5) and John Saunders (20).[2] Matthew Heath seems to have left the partnership to set himself up in business for on the 25th of March 1869 the Knights leased to him the old Wolverley Forges and certain premises at Cookley.[3] These properties had been previously leased to Henry Saunders Jnr. from the 24th of March 1860.[4]

The managing partner at Cookley was now John Saunders of Honeybrooke House. He, along with W. Piper of the Cookley Works, had patented during the 1860s a new process for tinning using what became known as the Cookley 'K' tin pot.[5] The tinplate trade at this time was pretty buoyant with home demand rising from 12,000 tons in 1860 to 84,000 tons in 1880. Exports of tinplate from Britain also rose during this period from 25,000 tons to 217,000 tons.[6] The United States of America proved to be the largest market for the export of British tinplate although setbacks did occur with financial crises in the country and with the American Civil War disrupting imports. However, depressions in the British tinplate industry tended to be short and recovery swift. The use of tinplate was spreading and there was a great demand for the product for food canning.

There were, however, problems developing with the wrought iron side of the business. There was a depression in the British iron industry in the late 1860s followed by a short lived boom in the early 1870s. This was a prelude to a great decline in the British iron trade. This occurred from the mid-1870s onwards and was the result of the rise of steel making and competition from foreign iron industries. Cookley, during the early 1870s, was operating 18 puddling furnaces for the manufacture of wrought iron.[7] A loss of about £2,700 was made during L.1877-78 and at this point the Knights invited Saunders to increase his shares in the company by buying them out. His reply in April 1879 was not optimistic as he wrote,

*Plate Seven* *The Cookley Iron and Tinplate Works photographed in the 1880s (photo courtesy Parkfield Steel Wheels)*

*Plate Eight* *The Cookley Iron and Tinplate Works photographed derelict in the 1890s (photo courtesy Parkfield Steel Wheels)*

> *The future of the iron trade is so involved in uncertainty that I would well to consider the question before deciding on the matter.*

The year L.1878-79 produced for the company a loss of about £8,400 with Saunders commenting,

> *It is hardly worth my giving an opinion on these times of change, rendered more uncertain by the extraordinary progress in the manufacture of steel.*[8]

The result of this uncertainty was that both the Knights and Saunders attempted to sell their shares. At the back of both sides' minds, however, must have been the idea that an opportunity existed to acquire total control of Cookley at a bargain price. First Saunders offered to sell his shares, stating his intent not to introduce his sons into the partnership. The Knights declined the offer giving the depressed state of the iron trade as their reason. Saunders then offered to buy the Knight shares in the company. This offer was rejected. Matters dragged on into 1880 when a scheme for the complete sale of Cookley as a going concern to an outside party or parties was mooted. Saunders seemed to be financially in a tight spot. The Knights calculated that with his 1/4 share in the tin pot patent, a 1/10 fee for managing the patent business and his share of Cookley profits he received £37,291 between 1866 and 1880. The Knights commented,

> *This with £1,000 a year salary would have made Saunders well off if Saunders and his family had not been very expensive in their mode of living.*[9]

The scheme to sell Cookley was a non-starter. Saunders correctly believed that the bar iron trade had gone from South Staffordshire. He firmly believed that the staple trade (wrought iron) had left the district and he used Baldwins' works at Broadwater as an example, for the works had ceased making wrought iron to make sheet and tinplate only. Cookley at this time had three tin mills, two sheet iron mills, a bar iron mill and a wire mill. The bar iron and wire mills were not even working a third of the time and were being used for only three full turns a week out of ten. These conditions must have carried on through to 1882 when the parish magazine commented on the depressed state of Cookley.[10] The iron and tinplate trades of the Kidderminster area were closely connected to the fortunes of the Black Country region. The Black Country iron industry was in serious decline and with that, the death of the wrought iron trade was imminent. In 1854 there had been 145 furnaces in blast in the Black Country and this figure had dropped to 45 in 1880.[11]

The ownership problem at Cookley was soon resolved with the deaths of C.A.Knight in 1879, John Saunders in 1881 and E.L.Knight in 1882. The death of Saunders forced Frederic Winn Knight into the position of managing partner although he commented that previously he had taken no interest in the management of the works.[12] Not only did Frederick Knight become the manager but also in 1882 he became the only surviving partner. So at the age of sixty nine Frederic Knight was pitchforked into the management of the Cookley Iron and Tinplate Works. He was the eldest son of John Knight and was educated at Charterhouse. At around the age of twenty nine he took over the management of the Knight estates on Exmoor and at first he employed no agent but undertook the task alone. Frederic Knight appears to have been a man of great determination and almost boundless energy. In the same year that he took over the management of the Exmoor estates he was elected Member of Parliament for West Worcestershire. He represented the constituency for forty four years and while an M.P. he was Parliamentary Secretary to the Poor Law Board in 1852 under Lord Derby's administration and again in 1858-59 under Lord Palmerston. Frederic Knight did have some commercial experience before the management of Cookley as in 1856 he became a director of the Bank of London and National Provincial Insurance Association.[13]

Frederic Knight seems to have kept the Cookley business going in the same manner as under the management of Saunders. On L.1884 stocks at Cookley included pig and refined iron, charcoal wire, charcoal stamped iron, best puddled bars, boiled pig bars, Swedish charcoal iron, coke bars, best best wrought iron, best wrought iron, charcoal sheets, tinplate, blackplate and terne.[14] It could well be that at this time tinplate sales were keeping the business afloat for exports of British tinplate had risen from 217,700 tons in 1880 to 448,379 tons in 1891.[15]

There was one irritation that Frederic Winn Knight had to contend with in 1884 when Sir John Sebright sold the Cookley land lease, under Lord Cairn's Act, to W. Green of Kidderminster.[16] What was even more annoying was that in order to secure a buyer for the lease a full description of the works was included in the auction details. However, this document gives us valuable details about the nature and state of the works in 1884. The Cookley Iron and Tinplate Works was described in the following manner,

> A - Pattern stores and office, two storeys high, built with cinder bricks and tiled.
>
> B - Pattern shop and stores, two storeys high, brick built and tiled.
>
> C - Foundry and two iron melting furnaces, brick built and tiled.
>
> D - Cottage, two storeys high, built with cinder brick and tiled and containing four rooms. It is known as the Stop House (entrance into sluice from canal).
>
> E - Brick store, built with cinder bricks and sheet iron roof.
>
> F - Boat builders shed.
>
> G - Warehouse, brick built and slated and paved with Staffordshire square fluted blue bricks. Canal sluice and wharf for unloading pig iron, coal etc. with weighing machine.
>
> H - Yards for storing charcoal.
>
> I - A two storey brick built and slated building containing on the upper floor a fitting shop and store room and on the ground floor a roll turning shop and blacksmith's shop, fitted with four hearths.
>
> K - Refinery fire and engine house.
>
> L - Charcoal fires (six).
>
> M - Merchant mill and merchant mill engine, puddle balls rolls and yard, six puddling furnaces. a further six puddling furnaces, two stack puddling furnaces, stampers, hammer and waterwheel.

*Plate Nine* *The older parts of the present Cookley Works pictured alongside the Staffordshire and Worcestershire Canal*

*Plate Ten*

*The canal feeder into the Cookley Works crossed by a cast iron bridge dated 1871.*

N - Brick built and tiled central office in two floors and weighing machine. Large sheet mill, small sheet mill, engine house and three pairs of cold rolls, three sheet iron and two annealing furnaces, two large annealing furnaces and three sheet iron furnaces.
O - Range of buildings, brick built with part slated and part glazed roof, comprising pickling room, large and small tin house, terne pots, bran store, scurf house for tin and terne metal. Tin house with fitting shop over and bran store.
P - A low range of buildings, brick built with sheet iron roof, comprising store room and shears shop, box stores, tallow and palm oil stores etc. Copperas work comprising brick and tiled shed, wood shed with iron roof and boilers complete.
Q - Gasometer, two beds of retorts (with three single retorts in each bed) and three purifiers (one water, one lime and one charcoal). Small annealing furnace.
R - Brick built and slated building containing tin house, four tinplate stocks for making tinplates (melting and coating). Pickling room etc.
S - Nelson's Tin Mill and Wellington Tin Mill (worked with one engine), engine house, shear shops and seven furnaces complete.
Bang-up tin mill, engine house and forge, roll turning shop, two pairs cold rolls, two heating furnaces and one puddling furnace, one cinder furnace and one puddling furnace.
T - Wire rolling mill, furnaces (two) and boiler.
U - Debdale Forge, four puddling furnaces, two heating furnaces with rolls and hammer complete. One double hollow fire, one single hollow fire and a patent hammer.
V - Old cottages, used as stores, lime shed, gasometer and puddlers' stack.
W - A range of buildings, brick built and iron roofed comprising carpenters' shop, saw mill fitted with three circular saws, saw pit, engine and boiler.
X - A range of brick buildings with semicircular brick roofs comprising blacksmiths' shop (two hearths), store room etc.
Y - A two storey brick built and tiled cottage containing six rooms.
Z - General offices, two storeys high, brick built and slated, comprising an upper floor, manager's private, cashiers and general offices, long room used as store room, lavatories etc. On ground floor, shipping clerks' and weighing machine offices etc.

Various castings including four waterwheels weighing,
(a) 5 ton 16 cwt 2 qrs 0 lbs
(b) 13 ton 6 cwt 2 qrs 2 lbs
(c) 9 ton 11 cwt 0 qrs 0 lbs
(d) 6 ton 0 cwt 0 qrs 0 lbs

A yearly tenancy because of a change of partnership at £325 per annum.[17]

The change of lease holder was a minor problem compared with the decline of the fortunes of the Cookley Works. The causes at the root of this decline affected other tinplate and sheet producers along the Stour. Another Stour manufacturer, E.P.& W. Baldwin of the Wilden and Swindon Sheet Iron and Tinplate Works wanted to increase production but decided to do this by erecting a new works in 1886 close to a supply of steel at Newport, Monmouthshire.[18] Certainly the writing was on the wall for works like Cookley.

Frederic Winn Knight was knighted in 1886 for public service as a Member of Parliament and a Justice of the Peace. He seems to have inherited the family trait of making bold decisions for in the same year as he received his knighthood he decided to remove the business from Cookley to Brockmoor, Brierley Hill.[19] The advantages of this move would be that the new works would have a rail link and would be situated in the centre of the Earl of Dudley's thick coalfield. The Cookley site was also getting rather constrained and cluttered with buildings, some of rather an ancient vintage. An indication of the age of the premises is shown by the names of some of the buildings, for at Cookley were Nelson's and Wellington tin mills and the Debdale Forge. The motive power in the works was provided by old fashioned beam steam engines and possibly by four waterwheels.[20]

The Brockmoor Works was operated by a new limited company and manufacture began there in around April 1886.[21] The complete transfer of machinery took some time and parts of the Cookley Works continued in production until early 1887 when the final portion of the move was completed.[22] The Cookley site remained unoccupied for several years and the buildings became derelict. In 1904 the site was acquired by F.W.Brampton who traded as the Chaddesley Manufacturing Co. Ltd. Amongst the products of the Chaddesley Manufacturing Co. were 'Dreadnought' steel wheels for road vehicles. The name of the operating company was changed in 1913 to Steel Stampings Ltd., and output of steel wheels for heavy commercial vehicles, tractors and agricultural machinery continued.[23] The Cookley Works is now operated by Parkfield Pressings & Fabrications, Steel Wheels, and manufacturing of ferrous products continues at this historic site which has witnessed the making of iron and steel products for virtually an unbroken run of over three hundred years.

The new Knight partnership was soon producing tinplate at Brockmoor, and in July 1886 it was forecast that in two months time two large sheet mills and a further tinning pot would be completed.[24] The tinning pot was an important part of the tinplating operation which had radically improved since the early Bringewood era. The first part of the operation was to roll wrought iron or steel bars into thin blackplate. The plates were then cleaned by being immersed in sulphuric acid. This cleaning process was called black pickling. The plates after pickling were annealed. This was carried out by the plates being packed into a cast iron box about two feet square from which air was excluded by luting on the cover. Several of these boxes were placed in a kind of reverberatory furnace where for twelve hours the plates were maintained at a cherry red heat. The heat was sufficient to make the plates adhere to each other and then after cooling they were cold rolled. The plates were

*Plate Eleven The older parts of the present Cookley Works.*

*Plate Twelve* *The old cottage that made up part of the old Cookley Works.*

then subjected to a second pickling, the so called white pickle. On withdrawal the plates were ready for the tinning operation.

The tinning apparatus consisted of a range of six pots placed over suitable fires. They were called respectively the tinman's pot, the tin pot, the washing pot (divided into two compartments), the grease pot, the cold pot and the list pot. The plates were first immersed in the melted grease of the tinman's pot until all the moisture had evaporated from the surfaces. They were then introduced into the molten tin contained in the tin pot, the surface of which was covered by a layer of grease. The plates were then transferred to the first division of the wash pot which also contained molten tin and here the plates remained until the coating was perfect and the excess tin had run off. To help rid the plates of excess tin a workman wiped both sides of the plate with a hemp brush and then to remove the streaks left by the hemp the plate was quickly dipped into the second division of the wash pot containing the purest tin. The Cookley modification of this process was that a set of rolls was fixed to the wash pot and surplus tin was removed not by brushing but by passing the plates through the rollers. The plates were then taken to the grease pot containing molten grease maintained at a heat to allow the excess tin to run off and allow the plate to cool uniformly without unequal contraction. After ten minutes' immersion in the grease pot the plates were put into molten tallow contained in the cold pot. To remove the bead or wire edge of tin which had collected on the lower edge of the plate it was inserted into the list pot which contained about 1⁄4 of an inch of molten tin at a moderately high temperature. The wire edge then melted and was removed by striking the plate sharply with a stick. The plates were then rubbed down with bran to clean off grease and dirt and then polished with a sheep skin.[25]

The move to Brockmoor and the new tinning plant must have needed a large additional investment in the company. Unfortunately the fortunes of the British tinplate industry were to receive a severe set back when in 1891 the Mckinley Tariff was introduced in the United States of America.[26] This greatly restricted the export of tinplate to America. The resulting depression in the tinplate industry was probably the reason why the Brockmoor Works amalgamated with the Stour Vale Works of Crowther Brothers. The new company took the title of Knight & Crowther Ltd.[27] Sir Frederic Knight died in 1897 but there appears to have been a Knight presence in the company until about 1902 when the two works were sold to Baldwins Limited.[28] This ended the Knight family's involvement with a trade which stretched from the seventeenth century into the early years of the twentieth century. The family's story is also the story of the progress of the British iron industry during the industrial revolution. It is a story unparalleled in the annals of the British iron trade.[29]

**References.**

1. K.P.L., K.M.,7477, Lease of Wolverley Wire Mill, 1857. This lease was destroyed during a flood but details are contained in the hand list for the Knight Manuscripts at Kidderminster Library.
2. K.P.L., K.M., 7393, Cookley Arbitration, 11th September 1888.

3. K.P.L., K.M., 6871, Lease of 25th March 1869.
4. K.P.L., K.M., 6866, Lease of 24th March 1860.
5. L.J.Thompson, *Guide to Cookley and Wolverley*, 1902, p.17.
6. W.E.Minchinton, *The British Tinplate Industry - A History*, Oxford, 1957, pp. 26-28.
7. S. Griffiths, *Griffiths' Guide to the Iron Trade of Great Britain*, 1873, p. 272.
8. K.P.L., K.M., 7731, Copies of letters and conversations with John Saunders made by the Knights.
9. K.P.L., K.M., 7339, Notes on conversations with John Saunders made by the Knights.
10. Betty Caswell, *A Scrapbook of Cookley Memories*, Cookley, 1989, p. 60.
11. W.K.V.Gale, *The Black Country Iron Industry*, 1979, pp. 138-139.
12. K.P.L., K.M., 7393, Cookley Arbitration, 11th September 1888.
13. C.S.Orwin & R.J.Sellick, *The Reclamation of Exmoor Forest*, Newton Abbot, 1970, pp. 32-33.
14. K.P.L., K.M., 7333, Financial accounts L.1883-84.
15. W.E.Minchinton. op. cit., p. 28.
16. K.P.L., K.M., 7393, Cookley Arbitration, 11th September 1888.
17. Sale Document of Cookley Iron and Tinplate Works, 18th September 1884.
18. *The Engineer*, January 29th 1886, p. 93.
19. K.P.L., K.M., 7393, Cookley Arbitration 11th September 1888.
20. K.P.L., K.M., 7393, Cookley Arbitration 11th September 1888.
21 *The Engineer*, April 16th 1886, p. 308.
22. *The Engineer*, July 16th 1886, p. 59.
23. Parkfield Steel Wheels, Cookley Works, Certificate of Change of Name for the Chaddesley Manufacturing Co. Ltd. to Steel Stampings Ltd., 26 July 1913.
24. *The Engineer*, July 16th 1886, p. 59.
25. W.H.Greenwood, *A Manual of Metallurgy*, Vol. 1, 1886, pp. 290-292.
26. W.E.Minchinton, op. cit., p. 44.
27. Betty Caswell, op. cit., p. 61.
28. R.Page, Richard and Edward Knight, Ironmasters of Bringewood and Wolverley, *Transactions of the Woolhope Naturalists' Field Club*, 43, 1981, p. 13.
29. The Cookley Works at Brockmoor as it became known continued in operation to become part of the strip products division of British Steel and, like the original Cookley Works, is still in existence.

# APPENDIX ONE.

Bringewood Ironworks - Output 1733-1779(1).

| Year | Furnace (tons) | Finery (tons) | Chafery (tons) | Tinworks (boxes) |
|---|---|---|---|---|
| M.1733-L.1734 | 584.75 | 248+1 | 218 | - |
| L.1734-35 | 0 | 312.5+11 | 313 | - |
| 1735-36 | 433.75 | 334 | 350 | - |
| 1736-37 | 0 | 318+17.5 | 330 | - |
| 1737-38 | 724 | 308 | 307 | - |
| 1738-39 | 0 | 316.5+14 | 331 | - |
| 1739-40 | 619.5 | 366.5 | 349 | - |
| 1740-41 | 0 | 284.25+19.25 | 313 | 270 |
| 1741-42 | 705 | 335 | 337 | 624 |
| 1742-43 | 0 | 364.75+4 | 354 | 1314 |
| 1743-44 | In blast | 358.25+9 | 379 | 1202 |
| 1744-45 | 189 | 387.5+13 | 387 | 1260 |
| 1745-46 | 941.5 | 398+4 | 403 | 1784.25 |
| 1746-47 | 0 | 421+5 | 409 | 1551.75 |
| 1747-48 | 123 | 355+21 | 400 | 1346 |
| 1748-49 | 752 | 378 | 377 | 1799.5 |
| 1749-50 | 0 | 368.5+20.5 | 395 | 1756.5 |
| 1750-51 | 701 | 403 | 415 | 2188.75 |
| 1751-52 | 0 | 431.75+1.25 | 432 | 2211.25 |
| 1752-53 | 714.5 | 444.5 | 409 | 2263.75 |
| 1753-54 | 0 | 329.5+2 | 352 | 1967.75 |
| 1754-55 | 597.75 | 352.75+30.75 | 390 | 1418 |
| 1755-56 | 0 | 400+18 | 426 | 2039.25 |
| 1756-57 | 694.75 | 419.5+27.5 | 443 | 2282.25 |
| 1757-58 | 598.1 | 405.5 | 407 | 2526 |
| 1758-59 | 524.5 | 447 | 451 | 2119 |
| 1759-60 | 436 | 379+35 | 412 | 2364 |
| 1760-61 | 258 | 380+24 | 399 | 2202.5 |

| Year | Furnace (tons) | Finery (tons) | Chafery (tons) | Tinworks (boxes) |
|---|---|---|---|---|
| 1761-62 | 382 | 409+17 | 405.15 | 2164 |
| 1762-63 | 430 | 349.5+14 | 399.9 | 1435.5 |
| 1763-64 | 435 | 336+10 | 341.9 | 1430 |
| 1764-65 | 468.75 | 407.5+17 | 409.7 | 1575.25 |
| 1765-66 | 324 | 372.5+17 | 453.65 | 1513 |
| 1766-67 | 562 | 506 | 508 | 1805.5 |
| 1767-68 | 386.5 | 487+28 | 510 | 1882.5 |
| 1768-69 | 484.3 | 496.5+15.5 | 490 | 2159.25 |
| 1769-70 | 660 | 483+15 | 519 | 2390.25 |
| 1770-71 | 485.15 | 510+17 | 525.15 | 1895 |
| 1771-72 | 524.85 | 456.5+31.5 | 407.35 | 1433 |
| 1772-73 | 143.35 | 520+15.5 | 476.4 | 1426.25 |
| 1773-74 | 851.85 | 446 | 432.45 | 1672 |
| 1774-75 | 293 | 370+21 | 453.1 | 608.5 |
| 1775-76 | 935.6 | 276 | 357.55 | 26 |
| 1776-77 | 0 | 458 | 457.4 | - |
| 1777-78 | 391 | 561 | 519 | - |
| 1778-79 | 653.5 | 469 | 465.5 | - |

* In all forge accounts the second figure in the finery output column relates to wrought iron made from broken iron and old castings.

SOURCE: K.P.L., K.M., General accounts of the Bringewood Partnership 1733-1779, No 244-282.

# APPENDIX TWO.

Bringewood Ironworks - Profit and Loss 1733-1779.

| Year | Furnace & Forge | Tinworks | Total |
|---|---|---|---|
| M.1733-L.1734 | £2244.55 | - | - |
| L.1734-35 | £621.5 | - | - |
| 1735-36 | £1205.7 | - | - |
| 1736-37 | £86.35 | - | - |
| 1737-38 | £1750.15 | - | - |
| 1738-39 | £60.5 | - | - |
| 1739-40 | £2118.3 | - | - |
| 1740-41 | - | - | £756.7 |
| 1741-42 | - | - | £2108.5 |
| 1742-43 | - | - | £423.45 |
| 1743-44 | £2640.3 | £523.15 | £3163.45 |
| 1744-45 | £1378.25 | £520.8 | £1899.05 |
| 1745-46 | £2620.6 | £420.35 | £3040.95 |
| 1746-47 | £1026.25 | £459.15 | £1485.4 |
| 1747-48 | £743.9 | £272.35 | £1016.25 |
| 1748-49 | £1983.15 | £389.4 | £2372.55 |
| 1749-50 | £290.1 | £539.15 | £829.25 |
| 1750-51 | £1877.9 | £586.7 | £2464.6 |
| 1751-52 | £119.75 | £424.5 | £544.25 |
| 1752-53 | £2464.75 | £212.75 | £2677.5 |
| 1753-54 | -£76.6 | £642.65 | £566.05 |
| 1754-55 | £1950.8 | £130 | £2080.8 |
| 1755-56 | £227.2 | -£35.05 | £192.15 |
| 1756-57 | £2443.45 | £37.4 | £2480.85 |
| 1757-58 | £1588.35 | £270.4 | £1858.75 |
| 1758-59 | £1493.6 | -£75.95 | £1417.65 |
| 1759-60 | £1970.9 | £263.2 | £2234.1 |
| 1760-61 | £1903.3 | £371.35 | £2274.65 |

| Year | Furnace & Forge | Tinworks | Total |
|---|---|---|---|
| 1761-62 | £1174.85 | £210.95 | £1358.8 |
| 1762-63 | £393.1 | £161.3 | £554.4 |
| 1763-64 | £847.3 | £135.9 | £983.2 |
| 1764-65 | £2030.2 | £56.65 | £2086.85 |
| 1765-66 | £1003.65 | £57.65 | £1061.3 |
| 1766-67 | £2103.5 | £448.35 | £2551.85 |
| 1767-68 | £1148.45 | £536.2 | £1684.65 |
| 1768-69 | £1467.15 | £433.55 | £1900.7 |
| 1769-70 | £2975 | £353.25 | £3328.25 |
| 1770-71 | £1753.3 | £134.25 | £1887.55 |
| 1771-72 | £1321.6 | £252.05 | £1573.65 |
| 1772-73 | -£724.5 | £360.9 | -£363.6 |
| 1773-74 | -£707.9 | £269.65 | -£438.25 |
| 1774-75 | -£361.9 | £119.05 | -£242.85 |
| 1775-76 | £398.9 | £68.4 | £467.3 |
| 1776-77 | £487.85 | -£1.05 | £486.8 |
| 1777-78 | £484.95 | - | - |
| 1778-79 | £79.9 | - | - |

# APPENDIX THREE.

Bringewood Ironworks - Input Prices.

| Year | Charcoal per load | Ironstone per load | Coal per ton |
|---|---|---|---|
| M.1733-L.1734 | £1.25 | £0.875 | - |
| L.1734-35 | £1.28 | £0.99 | - |
| 1735-36 | £1.28 | £0.99 | - |
| 1736-37 | £1.21 | £0.98 | - |
| 1737-38 | £1.20 | £0.96 | - |
| 1738-39 | £1.25 | £0.98 | - |
| 1739-40 | £1.20 | £0.99 | - |
| 1740-41 | £1.18 | £0.99 | - |
| 1741-42 | £1.17 | - | - |
| 1742-43 | £1.16 | £1.00 | £0.49 |
| 1743-44 | £1.09 | £0.99 | £0.51 |
| 1744-45 | £1.25 | £1.01 | £0.62 |
| 1745-46 | £1.21 | £1.00 | £0.60 |
| 1746-47 | £1.26 | £1.00 | £0.59 |
| 1747-48 | £1.18 | £1.01 | - |
| 1748-49 | £1.26 | £0.99 | - |
| 1749-50 | £1.24 | £0.99 | £0.50 |
| 1750-51 | £1.30 | £0.99 | £0.62 |
| 1751-52 | £1.29 | £0.98 | - |
| 1752-53 | £1.31 | - | £0.65 |
| 1753-54 | £1.35 | £1.02 | £0.66 |
| 1754-55 | £1.66 | £1.03 | £0.68 |
| 1755-56 | £2.21 | £1.08 | £0.77 |
| 1756-57 | £2.23 | £1.22 | £0.77 |
| 1757-58 | £2.15 | £1.21 | £0.72 |
| 1758-59 | £2.19 | £1.07 | £0.67 |
| 1759-60 | £2.11 | £1.07 | £0.65 |
| 1760-61 | £1.98 | £1.07 | £0.65 |

| Year | Charcoal per load | Ironstone per load | Coal per ton |
|---|---|---|---|
| 1761-62 | £1.99 | £1.05 | £0.67 |
| 1762-63 | £1.97 | £1.05 | £0.68 |
| 1763-64 | £1.81 | £1.05 | £0.67 |
| 1764-65 | £2.05 | £1.05 | £0.67 |
| 1765-66 | £2.06 | £1.05 | £0.70 |
| 1766-67 | £2.23 | £1.09 | £0.68 |
| 1767-68 | £1.98 | £1.06 | £0.68 |
| 1768-69 | £2.22 | £1.14 | £0.70 |
| 1769-70 | £2.40 | £1.26 | £0.72 |
| 1770-71 | £2.48 | £1.30 | £0.73 |
| 1771-72 | £2.94 | £1.37 | £0.76 |
| 1772-73 | £2.89 | £1.51 | £0.75 |
| 1773-74 | £2.93 | £1.64 | £0.75 |
| 1774-75 | £2.78 | £1.72 | £0.70 |
| 1775-76 | £2.70 | £1.45 | £0.74 |
| 1776-77 | £2.57 | £1.59 | £0.74 |
| 1777-78 | £2.58 | £1.60 | £0.74 |
| 1778-79 | £2.68 | - | £0.73 |

# APPENDIX FOUR.

Charlcotte Furnace - 1733-1779(2).

| Year | Output (tons) | Charcoal cost (load) | Charcoal used per ton of iron made. (loads) | Profit/Loss |
|---|---|---|---|---|
| 1733-35 | 495 | £1.55 | 1.66 | £361.2 |
| L.1735-36 | 261 | £1.45 | 2.0 | £130.3 |
| 1736-37 | 420 | £1.40 | 2.08 | £223.7 |
| 1737-38 | 593 | £1.35 | 1.66 | £718.45 |
| 1738-39 | 504 | £1.40 | 2.0 | £355.2 |
| 1739-40 | 470 | £1.45 | 1.83 | £242.85 |
| 1740-41 | 503 | £1.35 | 1.92 | £311.55 |
| 1741-42 | 430 | £1.30 | 1.66 | £468.45 |
| 1742-43 | 479 | £1.35 | 1.66 | £392.4 |
| 1743-44 | 410 | £1.40 | 2.08 | £441.55 |
| 1744-45 | 46 | £1.40 | - | £398.15 |
| 1745-46 | 33 | £1.40 | - | £436 |
| 1746-47 | 692 | £1.45 | 1.83 | £805.75 |
| 1747-48 | 60 | £1.40 | 2.0 | -£445.75 |
| 1748-49 | 373 | £1.45 | 1.92 | £294.5 |
| 1749-50 | 763 | £1.45 | 2.0 | £470.7 |
| 1750-51 | 0 | £1.55 | - | -£566.4 |
| 1751-52 | 696 | £1.65 | 1.83 | £459.75 |
| 1752-53 | 0 | £1.70 | - | -£286.45 |
| 1753-54 | 649 | £1.75 | 1.83 | £489.35 |
| 1754-55 | 84 | £1.90 | 1.66 | -£79.9 |
| 1755-56 | 636 | £2.70 | 1.58 | £287.5 |
| 1756-57 | 500 | £2.80 | 1.33 | £226.9 |
| 1757-58 | 200 | £2.65 | 1.83 | -£51.95 |
| 1758-59 | 550 | £2.55 | 1.08 | £290.5 |
| 1759-60 | 284 | £2.55 | 1.5 | -£283.2 |

| Year | Output (tons) | Charcoal cost (load) | Charcoal used per ton of iron made. (loads) | Profit/Loss |
|---|---|---|---|---|
| 1760-61 | 0 | £2.45 | - | -£367.5 |
| 1761-62 | 410 | £2.30 | 1.5 | -£472.95 |
| 1762-63 | 430 | £2.25 | 1.83 | -£86.85 |
| 1763-64 | 0 | £2.25 | - | -£355.5 |
| 1764-65 | 553 | £2.05 | 1.83 | £151.3 |
| 1765-66 | 471 | £2.30 | 1.66 | £205.7 |
| 1766-67 | 440 | £2.30 | 1.58 | -£21.5 |
| 1767-68 | 0 | £2.30 | - | -£418.55 |
| 1768-69 | 368 | £2.75 | 1.92 | -£560.55 |
| 1769-70 | 0 | £2.75 | - | -£70.65 |
| 1770-71 | 393 | £2.75 | 1.5 | -£327.85 |
| 1771-72 | 0 | £2.80 | - | -£321.35 |
| 1772-73 | 428 | £2.80 | 1.42 | -£49.65 |
| 1773-74 | 0 | £2.75 | - | -£138.6 |
| 1774-75 | 0 | £2.95 | - | -£252.85 |
| 1775-76 | 0 | £2.15 | - | - |
| 1776-77 | 575 | £2.30 | 1.58 | £96.3 |
| 1777-78 | 0 | £2.10 | - | - |
| 1778-79 | 0 | £2.35 | - | - |

These accounts run from Ladyday of one year to Ladyday of the next except for the first entry which represents the accounts from Midsummer, 1733, to, Ladyday, 1735.

SOURCES: K.P.L., K.M., General accounts of the Bringewood Partnership, 1733-1779,, No., 244-282., Norman, Mutton, Charlcot, Furnace, 1733-1779,, Historical, Metallurgy, Group Bulletin,, 1966,, pp., 45-53.

# APPENDIX FIVE.

Hales Furnace - 1726-1773.

| Year | Output (tons) | Ironstone cost per load | Charcoal cost per load | Charcoal needed to make a ton of iron (loads) |
|---|---|---|---|---|
| L.1726-27 | 477.3 | £0.59 | £2.13 | 2.44 |
| 1727-28 | 525.55 | £0.60 | £2.40 | 2.12 |
| 1728-30(3) | 712.5 | £0.65 | £2.42 | 2.17 |
| 1730-31 | 724.15 | £0.61 | £2.17 | 2.06 |
| 1731-32 | 630 | £0.61 | £2.0 | 2.23 |
| 1732-33 | 514.1 | £0.64 | £1.93 | 2.10 |
| 1733-34 | 490.3 | £0.65 | £1.69 | 2.25 |
| 1734-35 | 649.45 | £0.65 | £1.61 | 2.40 |
| 1735-36 | 347.4 | £0.66 | £1.68 | 2.29 |
| 1736-37 | 321.5 | £0.60 | £1.53 | 2.33 |
| 1737-38 | 609.4 | £0.68 | £1.63 | 2.01 |
| 1738-39 | 699 | £0.67 | £1.61 | 2.15 |
| 1739-40 | 177.4 | £0.68 | £1.62 | 2.17 |
| 1740-41 | 780.8 | £0.67 | £1.64 | 2.12 |
| 1741-42 | 570.15 | £0.67 | £1.66 | 2.13 |
| 1742-43 | 753.3 | £0.67 | £1.56 | 2.12 |
| 1743-44 | 632.8 | £0.66 | £1.54 | 2.12 |
| 1744-45 | 758.6 | £0.60 | £1.42 | 2.08 |
| 1745-46 | 0 | £0.59 | £1.60 | - |
| 1746-47 | 575.7 | £0.72 | £1.53 | 2.03 |
| 1747-48 | 0 | £0.66 | £1.57 | - |
| 1748-49 | 517.4 | £0.68 | £1.64 | 2.15 |
| 1749-50 | 0 | £0.80 | £1.53 | - |
| 1750-51 | 739.35 | £0.73 | £1.60 | 2.08 |
| 1751-52 | 79 | £0.72 | £1.67 | 2.11 |
| 1752-53 | 666.15 | £0.70 | £1.75 | 2.11 |

| Year | Output (tons) | Ironstone cost per load | Charcoal cost per load | Charcoal needed to make a ton of iron (loads) |
|---|---|---|---|---|
| 1753-54 | 148.1 | £0.71 | £1.72 | 2.12 |
| 1754-55 | 392.35 | - | £1.85 | 2.11 |
| 1755-56 | 593.55 | £0.78 | £2.03 | 2.12 |
| 1756-57 | 117 | £0.82 | £2.14 | 2.12 |
| 1757-58 | 821 | £0.81 | £2.16 | 2.0 |
| 1758-59 | 624.9 | £0.79 | £2.16 | 1.85 |
| 1759-60 | 0 | £0.77 | - | - |
| 1760-61 | 475 | £0.76 | £2.05 | 2.16 |
| 1761-62 | 0 | £0.78 | £2.05 | - |
| 1762-63 | 582 | £0.84 | £1.89 | 2.05 |
| 1763-64 | 66 | £0.68 | £1.76 | 1.99 |
| 1764-65 | 425.55 | £0.90 | £1.83 | 2.04 |
| 1765-66 | 159 | £0.85 | £1.97 | 2.12 |
| 1766-67 | 509.6 | £0.64 | £1.94 | 2.01 |
| 1767-68 | 0 | £0.72 | £1.91 | - |
| 1768-69 | 121.25 | £0.74 | £2.08 | 2.22 |
| 1769-70 | 0 | - | £2.16 | - |
| 1770-71 | 0 | - | £1.97 | - |
| 1771-72 | 248 | £0.79 | £2.20 | 1.94 |
| 1772-73 | Sale of remaining pigs. | - | - | - |

# APPENDIX SIX.

Aston Furnace - 1746-1784.

| Year | Output (tons) | Ironstone cost per load | Charcoal cost per load | Charcoal needed to make a ton of iron (loads) |
|---|---|---|---|---|
| L.1746-47 | 279.05 | - | £1.77 | - |
| 1747-48 | 409.6 | £0.62 | £1.66 | 2.03 |
| 1748-49 | 60.05 | £0.76 | £1.82 | 2.0 |
| 1749-50 | 716.8 | £0.70 | £1.75 | 1.96 |
| 1750-51 | 958 | £0.72 | £1.80 | 2.12 |
| 1751-52 | 990 | £0.72 | £1.76 | 1.86 |
| 1752-53 | 552 | £0.73 | £1.74 | 2.09 |
| 1753-54 | 819 | £0.73 | £1.89 | 1.77 |
| 1754-55 | 890 | £0.75 | £1.94 | 1.87 |
| 1755-56 | 486.5 | £0.75 | £2.07 | 2.02 |
| 1756-57 | 624.8 | £0.78 | £2.32 | 2.0 |
| 1757-58 | 904 | £0.79 | £2.23 | 2.0 |
| 1758-59 | 1027 | £0.76 | £2.14 | 1.77 |
| 1759-60 | 768.5 | £0.75 | £2.08 | 2.04 |
| 1760-61 | 930 | £0.75 | £2.12 | 1.96 |
| 1761-62 | 283 | £0.75 | £2.09 | 2.0 |
| 1762-63 | 781 | - | £2.0 | 1.98 |
| 1763-64 | 1041 | £0.83 | £1.82 | 1.97 |
| 1764-65 | 25.5 | £0.84 | £1.99 | 2.01 |
| 1765-66 | 824.45 | £0.87 | £2.08 | 1.86 |
| 1766-67 | 36 | £0.77 | £2.09 | 2.01 |
| 1767-68 | 972 | £0.75 | £2.11 | 1.92 |
| 1768-69 | 635 | £0.75 | £2.15 | 1.83 |
| 1769-70 | 0 | £0.89 | £2.14 | - |
| 1770-71 | 697 | £0.82 | £2.13 | 2.07 |
| 1771-72 | 281.7 | £0.79 | £2.27 | 2.01 |

| Year | Output (tons) | Ironstone cost per load | Charcoal cost per load | Charcoal needed to make a ton of iron (loads) |
|---|---|---|---|---|
| 1772-73 | 0 | £0.76 | £2.21 | - |
| 1773-74 | 869 | £0.81 | £2.12 | 1.92 |
| 1774-75 | 635 | £0.81 | £1.96 | 1.83 |
| 1775-76 | 0 | £0.81 | £1.78 | - |
| 1776-77 | 0 | £0.81 | £1.74 | - |
| 1777-78 | 98 | - | - | - |
| 1778-79 | 957 | £0.95 | £1.92 | 2.0 |
| 1779-80 | 194 | £0.84 | £1.71 | 2.03 |
| 1780-81 | 0 | £0.85 | £1.67 | - |
| 1781-82 | 0 | £0.86 | £1.63 | - |
| 1782-83 | 851 | - | £1.80 | - |
| 1783-84 | 184.7 | - | £1.81 | - |

# APPENDIX SEVEN.

The Price of One Ton of Pig Iron from Hales, Aston and Bringewood Furnaces.

| Year | Hales | Aston | Bringewood |
|---|---|---|---|
| L.1726-27 | £8.5 | - | - |
| 1727-28 | £8.54 | - | - |
| 1728-29 | £8.17 | - | - |
| 1729-30 | £7.71 | - | - |
| 1730-31 | £7.10 | - | - |
| 1731-32 | £7.06 | - | - |
| 1732-33 | £6.70 | - | - |
| 1733-34 | £6.50 | - | - |
| 1734-35 | £6.0 | - | £7.27 |
| 1735-36 | £6.20 | - | £7.01 |
| 1736-37 | £6.20 | - | £6.71 |
| 1737-38 | £6.20 | - | £6.50 |
| 1738-39 | £6.20 | - | £6.34 |
| 1739-40 | £6.20 | - | £6.36 |
| 1740-41 | £6.30 | - | £6.25 |
| 1741-42 | £6.25 | - | £6.25 |
| 1742-43 | £6.20 | - | £6.50 |
| 1743-44 | £5.90 | - | £5.63 |
| 1744-45 | £5.70 | - | £5.75 |
| 1745-46 | £5.75 | - | £5.75 |
| 1746-47 | £6.0 | £6.30 | £5.75 |
| 1747-48 | £6.37 | £6.40 | £5.75 |
| 1748-49 | £6.50 | £6.50 | £5.75 |
| 1749-50 | £6.25 | £6.65 | £6.0 |
| 1750-51 | £6.25 | £6.35 | £6.02 |
| 1751-52 | £6.25 | £6.35 | £6.65 |
| 1752-53 | £6.50 | £6.35 | £6.62 |

| Year | Hales | Aston | Bringewood |
|---|---|---|---|
| 1753-54 | £7.0 | £7.0 | £6.75 |
| 1754-55 | £7.62 | £7.50 | £7.90 |
| 1755-56 | £7.87 | £7.75 | £7.90 |
| 1756-57 | £7.87 | £7.50 | £7.90 |
| 1757-58 | £7.87 | £7.41 | £8.0 |
| 1758-59 | £7.87 | £7.52 | £8.0 |
| 1759-60 | £7.12 | £7.0 | £7.75 |
| 1760-61 | £7.12 | £7.0 | £7.75 |
| 1761-62 | £7.12 | £7.0 | £7.75 |
| 1762-63 | £7.12 | £7.0 | £7.75 |
| 1763-64 | £7.12 | £7.0 | £7.75 |
| 1764-65 | £7.12 | £7.0 | £7.75 |
| 1765-66 | £7.12 | £7.0 | £7.75 |
| 1766-67 | £7.12 | £7.0 | £7.75 |
| 1767-68 | £7.12 | £7.0 | £7.75 |
| 1768-69 | £7.12 | £7.0 | £7.75 |
| 1769-70 | £7.12 | £7.0 | £7.75 |
| 1770-71 | £7.12 | £7.0 | £7.75 |
| 1771-72 | £6.65 | £7.0 | £7.75 |
| 1772-73 | - | - | £7.50 |
| 1773-74 | - | £6.0 | £7.50 |
| 1774-75 | - | £6.0 | £7.50 |
| 1775-76 | - | - | £8.0 |
| 1776-77 | - | £6.10 | £8.98 |
| 1777-78 | - | £6.10 | £9.26 |
| 1778-79 | - | £6.0 | £8.61 |
| 1779-80 | - | £6.10 | - |
| 1780-81 | - | £6.10 | - |
| 1781-82 | - | £6.10 | - |
| 1782-83 | - | £6.10 | - |
| 1783-84 | - | £6.10 | - |

# APPENDIX EIGHT.

Wolverley Forge - 1727-1800.

| Year | Output of finery (tons) | Output of chafery (tons) | Charcoal cost per load | Charcoal used (loads) |
|---|---|---|---|---|
| 1727-28(4) | 21 | 20.5 | £2.02 | - |
| L.1728-29 | 250.5+2.5 | 255.5 | £1.92 | 444.5 |
| 1729-30 | 203.5+3.5 | 210.55 | £1.80 | 361.5 |
| 1730-31 | 228 | 231.1 | £1.84 | 572.12 |
| 1731-32 | 250+9.5 | 267.4 | £1.74 | 435.25 |
| 1732-33 | 239.5+1.5 | 251.55 | £1.61 | 421 |
| 1733-34 | 254.5+9 | 277.25 | £1.55 | 519.62 |
| 1734-35 | 254 | 229 | £1.46 | 458.5 |
| 1735-36 | 244+10 | 250.85 | £1.45 | 447.75 |
| 1736-37 | 238.5+3 | 290.75 | £1.38 | 422.5 |
| 1737-38 | 292 | 292.6 | £1.30 | 509.75 |
| 1738-39 | 242.25+6 | 301.75 | £1.37 | 434.75 |
| 1739-40 | 290.25+9.75 | 345.35 | £1.46 | 522.62 |
| 1740-41 | 294 | 283.3 | £1.43 | 500 |
| 1741-42 | 305.5+9.5 | 318.9 | £1.39 | 542.87 |
| 1742-43 | 305.5+8 | 313.75 | £1.46 | 500.75 |
| 1743-44 | 300.5 | 283.55 | £1.44 | 478.62 |
| 1744-45 | 314 | 339.4 | £1.32 | 379.75 |
| 1745-46 | 266.5+11.5 | 302.4 | £1.51 | 386.25 |
| 1746-47 | 292 | 301.95 | £1.55 | 385.62 |
| 1747-48 | 272.5+11.5 | 280.2 | £1.52 | 386.5 |
| 1748-49 | 301.5+5 | 276.5 | £1.55 | 426 |
| 1749-50 | 300.5+5.5 | 317.25 | £1.63 | 434.37 |
| 1750-51 | 275+6.5 | 332.25 | £1.59 | 421.5 |
| 1751-52 | 252.5 | 258.45 | £1.62 | 393.62 |
| 1752-53 | 281+9 | 282 | £1.88 | 420.62 |
| 1753-54 | 323.5 | 343.45 | £1.71 | 464.75 |

| Year | Output of finery (tons) | Output of chafery (tons) | Charcoal cost per load | Charcoal used (loads) |
|---|---|---|---|---|
| 1754-55 | 285.5+9.5 | 303.7 | £1.89 | 436.75 |
| 1755-56 | 299 | 306.6 | £2.12 | 433.25 |
| 1756-57 | 300+10.5 | 318.2 | £2.08 | 475.25 |
| 1757-58 | 324+6.5 | 340.5 | £2.10 | 478 |
| 1758-59 | 302+8 | 327.6 | £2.20 | 429.75 |
| 1759-60 | 300.75+14.75 | 337.85 | £2.08 | 445.5 |
| 1760-61 | 289 | 316.85 | £2.07 | 415.25 |
| 1761-62 | 268.5+13.5 | 287.05 | £2.14 | 395.62 |
| 1762-63 | 272 | 311.35 | £2.01 | 390.25 |
| 1763-64 | 270.5+11 | 324.75 | £1.86 | 408.87 |
| 1764-65 | 287 | 299.35 | £1.82 | 432.25 |
| 1765-66 | 223.5+16 | 245.35 | £1.85 | 369.12 |
| 1766-67 | 274.5 | 306.9 | £1.79 | 454.5 |
| 1767-68 | 278+13 | 316.8 | £1.89 | 445.87 |
| 1768-69 | 259.5 | 272.35 | £2.06 | 408.25 |
| 1769-70 | 256.5+7 | 273.5 | £1.99 | 432.25 |
| 1770-71 | 272.5 | 343.5 | £2.03 | 480.37 |
| 1771-72 | 290.5+12 | 318 | £2.07 | 488.12 |
| 1772-73 | 299.25+14 | 328.75 | £2.06 | 570.87 |
| 1773-74 | 290.5 | 298.4 | £2.10 | 530 |
| 1774-75 | 306.5+7 | 324.75 | £2.08 | 498.62 |
| 1775-76 | 316+13.5 | 340.95 | £1.79 | 533.5 |
| 1776-77 | 309.5+18 | 338.6 | £1.79 | 554.87 |
| 1777-78 | 295.5+34 | 339.15 | £1.74 | 545.87 |
| 1778-79 | 347+1 | 371 | £1.82 | 566.87 |
| 1779-80 | 344+5 | 365.1 | £1.93 | 543.12 |
| 1780-81 | 348.5+2 | 359.45 | £1.99 | 527.12 |
| 1781-82 | 316+18.5 | 362.4 | £2.10 | 573.87 |
| 1782-83 | 309+23 | 378 | £2.19 | 569.25 |
| 1783-84 | 348+6 | 395.75 | £1.87 | 578.5 |
| 1784-85 | 339.5+8.5 | 368.65 | £1.84 | 566.12 |
| 1785-86 | 218+26 | 362.45 | £1.69 | 448 |
| 1786-87 | 345+6 | 419.5 | £1.73 | 588.5 |

| Year | Output of finery (tons) | Output of chafery (tons) | Charcoal cost per load | Charcoal used (loads) |
|---|---|---|---|---|
| 1787-88 | 331.5+9 | 414.6 | £1.75 | 519.62 |
| 1788-89 | 344+6 | 361.35 | £1.68 | 611.2 |
| 1789-90 | 304 | 331.75 | £1.80 | 531.49 |
| 1790-91 | 299+9.5 | 318.45 | £1.86 | 534.5 |
| 1791-92 | 297+5.7 | 312.15 | £2.04 | 505.62 |
| 1792-93 | 314+8 | 376.25+42 | £2.03 | 613 |
| 1793-94 | 231+6 | 257.85 | £2.05 | 759.75 |
| 1794-95 | 218.5+7.5 | 229.35 | £2.10 | 429 |
| 1795-96 | 156.5 | 187.15 | £2.16 | 275.12 |
| 1796-97 | 194.5+3.5 | 179.2 | £2.24 | 337.12 |
| 1797-98 | 319.5+10 | 344.6 | £2.42 | 526.25 |
| 1798-99 | 316+2 | 333 | £2.50 | 564.37 |
| 1799-1800 | 286.5+8 | 332 | £2.16 | 498 |

# APPENDIX NINE.

Cookley Forge - 1726-1801.

| Year | Output of finery (tons) | Output of chafery (tons) | Charcoal cost per load | Charcoal used (loads) |
|---|---|---|---|---|
| 1726-27 | 329 | 340.25 | £1.93 | 575.12 |
| 1727-28 | 151.75 | 161 | £2.17 | 265.37 |
| 1728-29 | 254 | 292.5 | £1.98 | 448.62 |
| 1729-30 | 201.5+5.5 | 212.7 | £1.88 | 361.5 |
| 1730-31 | 270 | 265.5 | £1.78 | 492.25 |
| 1731-32 | 252.5+14.5 | 281.9 | £1.79 | 455 |
| 1732-33 | 261 | 261.4 | £1.69 | 451.75 |
| 1733-34 | 260+20.55 | 281.9 | £1.54 | 472.12 |
| 1734-35 | 270.5 | 238.5 | £1.44 | 473.37 |
| 1735-36 | 230.5+18 | 278.8 | £1.51 | 401.12 |
| 1736-37 | 262.65+5 | 319.8 | £1.40 | 426.12 |
| 1737-38 | 311.5+3.5 | 340.6 | £1.34 | 551.25 |
| 1738-39 | 251.8+8.5 | 303.65 | £1.35 | 456.5 |
| 1739-40 | 291.6+8.5 | 340.35 | £1.46 | 522.62 |
| 1740-41 | 305 | 321.8 | £1.44 | 442.75 |
| 1741-42 | 313+8 | 326.05 | £1.52 | 562.12 |
| 1742-43 | 310 | 325 | £1.51 | 493.87 |
| 1743-44 | 274.5+12 | 304.35 | £1.47 | 441.37 |
| 1744-45 | 310.5 | 339.45 | £1.27 | 370.87 |
| 1745-46 | 298 | 339.3 | £1.37 | 449.87 |
| 1746-47 | 283.5+14 | 325.6 | £1.57 | 396 |
| 1747-48 | 290.5 | 295.45 | £1.50 | 368 |
| 1748-49 | 280+8 | 278.5 | £1.58 | 402.5 |
| 1749-50 | 290.5 | 338.55 | £1.61 | 399.5 |
| 1750-51 | 284+10.5 | 362.8 | £1.64 | 450.25 |
| 1751-52 | 303 | 318.25 | £1.60 | 467 |
| 1752-53 | 254.5 | 274.55 | £1.84 | 389.12 |

| Year | Output of finery (tons) | Output of chafery (tons) | Charcoal cost per load | Charcoal used (loads) |
|---|---|---|---|---|
| 1753-54 | 292.5+18 | 342.15 | £1.77 | 494 |
| 1754-55 | 275.5 | 285.55 | £1.88 | 429.99 |
| 1755-56 | 283+9 | 299.4 | £2.10 | 440.37 |
| 1756-57 | 292+10 | 309.8 | £2.07 | 495 |
| 1757-58 | 299+10 | 363.85 | £2.13 | 487 |
| 1758-59 | 248+12 | 362.35 | £2.25 | 406 |
| 1759-60 | 260.5+21 | 332.15 | £2.10 | 450.25 |
| 1760-61 | 295 | 324.85 | £2.09 | 466.25 |
| 1761-62 | 288+18 | 338 | £2.13 | 474.87 |
| 1762-63 | 257.5 | 304.6 | £2.01 | 418.25 |
| 1763-64 | 220+12.5 | 284 | £1.90 | 365.75 |
| 1764-65 | 291.5 | 326.3 | £1.89 | 471 |
| 1765-66 | 252.5+17 | 284.2 | £1.95 | 438.87 |
| 1766-67 | 257.5+12 | 339.55 | £1.82 | 467.75 |
| 1767-68 | 256+9.5 | 318.55 | £1.94 | 406.87 |
| 1768-69 | 276.5 | 304.55 | £2.04 | 441.62 |
| 1769-70 | 260+6 | 279.45 | £2.02 | 453.87 |
| 1770-71 | 251.25 | 275.75 | £2.17 | 431.62 |
| 1771-72 | 286.5+13 | 309.15 | £2.05 | 472.75 |
| 1772-73 | 306+12 | 341.1 | £2.14 | 533.25 |
| 1773-74 | 287 | 291.45 | £2.09 | 519.75 |
| 1774-75 | 292.5+9.5 | 324.5 | £2.09 | 504.75 |
| 1775-76 | 314+4.5 | 332.4 | £1.82 | 536.37 |
| 1776-77 | 318 | 322.25 | £1.82 | 497 |
| 1777-78 | 301.5+9 | 321.4 | £1.85 | 543.37 |
| 1778-79 | 305 | 340.85 | £1.82 | 506.37 |
| 1779-80 | 304.5+11 | 323.85 | £1.92 | 518 |
| 1780-81 | 294.5+6 | 340.55 | £1.94 | 537.5 |
| 1781-82 | 285+6.5 | 376.25 | £1.91 | 524.37 |
| 1782-83 | 272.5+6 | 346.5 | £1.98 | 516.12 |
| 1783-84 | 283+7 | 294 | £1.88 | 538.5 |
| 1784-85 | 266.15+23.85 | 334.1 | £1.82 | 520.37 |
| 1785-86 | 355+11.5 | 392.25 | £1.72 | 566.75 |

| Year | Output of finery (tons) | Output of chafery (tons) | Charcoal cost per load | Charcoal used (loads) |
|---|---|---|---|---|
| 1786-87 | 343.5+8 | 361.85 | £1.74 | 552.5 |
| 1787-88 | 366.5 | 367.3 | £1.71 | 581.5 |
| 1788-89 | 351+4 | 344.15 | £1.87 | 725.75 |
| 1789-90 | 354.5 | 368.45 | £1.93 | 649.75 |
| 1790-91 | 311+2 | 324.25 | £2.00 | 558.5 |
| 1791-92 | 326+5 | 332.1 | £2.05 | 532.5 |
| 1792-93 | 335.5+2 | 337.15 | £1.98 | 626.12 |
| 1793-94 | 289+11 | 299.35 | £2.16 | 514.62 |
| 1794-95 | 266.5+6 | 267.65 | £2.10 | 705.5 |
| 1795-96 | 290 | 297.65 | £2.06 | 509 |
| 1796-97 | 311 | 312.3 | £2.25 | 609.25 |
| 1797-98 | 315+6.6 | 346 | £2.39 | 404.62 |
| 1798-99 | 302.5+2.1 | 317.45 | £2.64 | 384.12 |
| 1799-1800 | 337 | 368.25 | £2.22 | 428.87 |
| 1800-01 | 282 | 327.5 | £2.15 | 306.37 |

# APPENDIX TEN.

Whittington Forge - 1726-1771.

| Year | Output of finery (tons) | Output of chafery (tons) | Charcoal cost per load | Charcoal used (loads) |
|---|---|---|---|---|
| L.1726-27 | 271 | 277.95 | £1.95 | 440.37 |
| 1727-28 | 219.25 | 232.85 | £1.85 | 375.25 |
| 1728-29 | 201.5+3.15 | 203 | £1.94 | 356 |
| 1729-30 | 196.75+4.5 | 206.1 | £1.79 | 351.5 |
| 1730-31 | 248.5 | 284.7 | £1.80 | 498.12 |
| 1731-32 | 249.5+13.5 | 243.75 | £1.78 | 422.37 |
| 1732-33 | 227.5+19.4 | 276.25 | £1.61 | 417.75 |
| 1733-34 | 268.7+7.5 | 270.15 | £1.60 | 482.62 |
| 1734-35 | 229.5+11 | 254.2 | £1.48 | 494 |
| 1735-36 | 237.5+6 | 281.45 | £1.48 | 383.62 |
| 1736-37 | 259.75+3.25 | 329.1 | £1.47 | 459.87 |
| 1737-38 | 295+2 | 321.55 | £1.37 | 519.5 |
| 1738-39 | 205 | 314.8 | £1.48 | 437.25 |
| 1739-40 | 288+15 | 333.35 | £1.32 | 528.87 |
| 1740-41 | 300.5 | 309.85 | £1.37 | 437.25 |
| 1741-42 | 250.5+20 | 297.5 | £1.40 | 462.12 |
| 1742-43 | 293+10.5 | 285.95 | £1.35 | 484.5 |
| 1743-44 | 277.25+9.25 | 320.5 | £1.39 | 463 |
| 1744-45 | 279+10 | 351.4 | £1.27 | 374.37 |
| 1745-46 | 278.5+9 | 330.2 | £1.40 | 418.75 |
| 1746-47 | 291.5 | 310.95 | £1.36 | 437.25 |
| 1747-48 | 269+11.75 | 305 | £1.43 | 379.5 |
| 1748-49 | 288+15 | 300.25 | £1.51 | 431 |
| 1749-50 | 299.5+10 | 322.8 | £1.50 | 451.5 |
| 1750-51 | 282+9.5 | 323.7 | £1.74 | 434.87 |
| 1751-52 | 286 | 296.45 | £1.66 | 438.75 |
| 1752-53 | 265+10.5 | 283.8 | £1.76 | 406.62 |

| Year | Output of finery (tons) | Output of chafery (tons) | Charcoal cost per load | Charcoal used (loads) |
|---|---|---|---|---|
| 1753-54 | 276+17 | 302.5 | £1.81 | 410.62 |
| 1754-55 | 281.5+6 | 298.55 | £1.80 | 430.12 |
| 1755-56 | 286.5+6 | 303.1 | £2.05 | 435 |
| 1756-57 | 264.5+10 | 295.4 | £2.04 | 462.75 |
| 1757-58 | 312+8.5 | 327.8 | £2.06 | 515.75 |
| 1758-59 | 297.5 | 313.95 | £2.09 | 474.5 |
| 1759-60 | 277+10 | 296.75 | £2.02 | 464.5 |
| 1760-61 | 244+9.5 | 285.25 | £1.91 | 430.12 |
| 1761-62 | 274 | 264.05 | £1.95 | 457.25 |
| 1762-63 | 259.5+8.5 | 279.6 | £1.89 | 435.5 |
| 1763-64 | 271.5+6 | 298.65 | £1.70 | 451.62 |
| 1764-65 | 280+1 | 295.35 | £1.66 | 428.62 |
| 1765-66 | 273.25+11 | 286 | £1.79 | 459.5 |
| 1766-67 | 262 | 279 | £1.75 | 456.62 |
| 1767-68 | 247.5+10 | 278 | £1.91 | 433.25 |
| 1768-69 | 216.5 | 262.3 | £1.99 | 342.25 |
| 1769-70 | 157.5+3.5 | 191.4 | £1.94 | 262.12 |
| 1770-71 | 175.5+4.5 | 196.5 | £1.97 | 291 |

# APPENDIX ELEVEN.

Mitton Lower Forge - 1734-1797.

| Year | Output of finery (tons) | Output of chafery (tons) | Charcoal cost per load | Charcoal used (loads) |
|---|---|---|---|---|
| 1734-35(5) | 188.15 | 167.25 | £1.42 | 354.75 |
| L.1735-36 | 355.5+9.5 | 289.1 | £1.41 | 639.62 |
| 1736-37 | 376.6+8.6 | 342.3 | £1.39 | 717 |
| 1737-38 | 435+7.25 | 379.75 | £1.41 | 773.4 |
| 1738-39 | 406.25 | 365.65 | £1.35 | 713.16 |
| 1739-40 | 448+15.5 | 395.9 | £1.27 | 811.62 |
| 1740-41 | 452.5 | 373.45 | £1.26 | 788.87 |
| 1741-42 | 369.25+12.25 | 358.8 | £1.30 | 668.87 |
| 1742-43 | 421 | 369.5 | £1.67 | 638 |
| 1743-44 | 424.5 | 370.75 | £1.41 | 744.12 |
| 1744-45 | 430.75 | 338.05 | £1.39 | 547.37 |
| 1745-46 | 423+22 | 396.35 | £1.47 | 679.75 |
| 1746-47 | 443.75 | 383.75 | £1.53 | 612.62 |
| 1747-48 | 423.25+14 | 387.5 | £1.51 | 601.75 |
| 1748-49 | 463.5 | 386.5 | £1.47 | 635.37 |
| 1749-50 | 426+17 | 410.9 | £1.56 | 608.87 |
| 1750-51 | 453.25 | 478.75 | £1.55 | 622.87 |
| 1751-52 | 399.25+22.25 | 427.33 | £1.75 | 558.25 |
| 1752-53 | 408.25 | 378.25 | £1.82 | 561.5 |
| 1753-54 | 441+13.5 | 427.6 | £1.79 | 427 |
| 1754-55 | 424.75 | 455.25 | £1.93 | 583 |
| 1755-56 | 444+15 | 479.25 | £2.20 | 639.37 |
| 1756-57 | 488 | 514.85 | £2.19 | 653.5 |
| 1757-58 | 468.5+32.5 | 500.9 | £2.14 | 693.75 |
| 1758-59 | 485.5 | 468.25 | £2.12 | 650.62 |
| 1759-60 | 485 | 485.05 | £2.22 | 652.87 |
| 1760-61 | 421.5+31.5 | 445 | £2.11 | 647.5 |

| Year | Output of finery (tons) | Output of chafery (tons) | Charcoal cost per load | Charcoal used (loads) |
|---|---|---|---|---|
| 1761-62 | 466 | 440 | £2.14 | 633.5 |
| 1762-63 | 438+17 | 447.25 | £2.08 | 626.87 |
| 1763-64 | 424.5+24 | 407 | £1.89 | 584.25 |
| 1764-65 | 482.5 | 499.5 | £2.11 | 663 |
| 1765-66 | 439.5+21 | 478 | £1.87 | 678 |
| 1766-67 | 481.5 | 446.5 | £1.92 | 723.12 |
| 1767-68 | 462.5 | 426.75 | £1.86 | 695.37 |
| 1768-69 | 440.5 | 502.75 | £2.10 | 674.87 |
| 1769-70 | 437 | 420.25 | £2.16 | 677.87 |
| 1770-71 | 387 | 398 | £2.36 | 616.12 |
| 1771-72 | 507 | 500.25 | £2.35 | 759.87 |
| 1772-73 | 442+31 | 494.5 | £2.15 | 712.75 |
| 1773-74 | 456 | 467.75 | £2.30 | 705 |
| 1774-75 | 488 | 495 | £2.17 | 736 |
| 1775-76 | 515.5+16.5 | 545.5 | £2.03 | 833.37 |
| 1776-77 | 551 | 567 | £1.80 | 826.37 |
| 1777-78 | 507.5+10.5 | 535.25 | £1.85 | 809.25 |
| 1778-79 | 479.5+7.5 | 529.5 | £1.89 | 741.75 |
| 1779-80 | 527.5 | 488.75 | £2.00 | 857.75 |
| 1780-81 | 477+12.5 | 527 | £2.04 | 803 |
| 1781-82 | 496.5 | 520.5 | £1.96 | 808.62 |
| 1782-83 | 472.5+11 | 557.4 | £2.11 | 806.62 |
| 1783-84 | 544.5+6 | 515 | £1.94 | 914.25 |
| 1784-85 | 493.5+7.5 | 429.5 | £1.76 | 849.25 |
| 1785-86 | 468.5+6 | 434 | £1.70 | 865.25 |
| 1786-87 | 426+7.5 | 517.25 | £1.65 | 806.87 |
| 1787-88 | 582.5+8.5 | 618 | £1.74 | 928.75 |
| 1788-89 | 514.5+7 | 547.75 | £1.73 | 903.37 |
| 1789-90 | 553 | 564.25 | £1.93 | 951.25 |
| 1790-91 | 476.5+10.5 | 489.5 | £2.11 | 812.12 |
| 1791-92 | 496.5+9 | 533.5 | £2.28 | 825.87 |
| 1792-93 | 511 | 523.25 | £2.33 | 862.25 |
| 1793-94 | 458 | 531.75 | £2.30 | 783.37 |

| Year | Output of finery (tons) | Output of chafery (tons) | Charcoal cost per load | Charcoal used (loads) |
|---|---|---|---|---|
| 1794-95 | 414 + 21 | 447.25 | £2.31 | 881.12 |
| 1795-96 | 439 + 12 | 473 | £2.38 | 795.87 |
| 1796-97 | 469 | 518.65 | £2.42 | 812.25 |

# APPENDIX TWELVE.

Mitton Upper Forge - 1740-1796.

| Year | Output of finery (tons) | Output of chafery (tons) | Charcoal cost per load | Charcoal used (loads) |
|---|---|---|---|---|
| 1740-41 | 326 | 306 | £1.28 | 650 |
| 1741-42 | 406.25 | 406.65 | £1.37 | 732.25 |
| 1742-43 | 441.25 | 407.95 | £1.40 | 752.87 |
| 1743-44 | 403 + 16.75 | 384.45 | £1.40 | 697.25 |
| 1744-45 | 390.5 | 497.35 | £1.34 | 574.12 |
| 1745-46 | 421.25 + 11.25 | 489.05 | £1.47 | 589.12 |
| 1746-47 | 466.75 | 473.65 | £1.51 | 640.87 |
| 1747-48 | 443.25 + 13.5 | 445.6 | £1.51 | 628.37 |
| 1748-49 | 493.5 | 481.75 | £1.48 | 677.87 |
| 1749-50 | 454 + 18 | 499 | £1.56 | 649.37 |
| 1750-51 | 443 | 522 | £1.57 | 608.62 |
| 1751-52 | 449 + 18 | 483.05 | £1.66 | 671.62 |
| 1752-53 | 424 | 457.85 | £1.78 | 609.57 |
| 1753-54 | 460 + 12.5 | 477.6 | £1.77 | 683.25 |
| 1754-55 | 451.25 | 467.6 | £1.89 | 604.37 |
| 1755-56 | 460 + 18 | 446.9 | £2.22 | 659.62 |
| 1756-57 | 496.75 | 489.45 | £2.12 | 752.62 |
| 1757-58 | 499.5 + 33.5 | 499.65 | £2.12 | 814.37 |
| 1758-59 | 537 | 501 | £2.12 | 696.87 |
| 1759-60 | 499.5 | 475.3 | £2.16 | 704.87 |
| 1760-61 | 487.5 + 28 | 488.75 | £2.14 | 725 |
| 1761-62 | 451 | 478.5 | £2.03 | 652.5 |
| 1762-63 | 458.5 + 17 | 424.3 | £1.95 | 721.62 |
| 1763-64 | 500 | 505 | £1.95 | 726 |
| 1764-65 | 528 | 509.5 | £2.05 | 725.62 |
| 1765-66 | 444 + 18 | 442 | £1.82 | 780.75 |
| 1766-67 | 479.5 | 369 | £1.80 | 823.25 |

| Year | Output of finery (tons) | Output of chafery (tons) | Charcoal cost per load | Charcoal used (loads) |
|---|---|---|---|---|
| 1767-68 | 490.5 | 463 | £1.88 | 754.75 |
| 1768-69 | 467.5 | 479.75 | £2.04 | 755.62 |
| 1769-70 | 423 | 431.6 | £2.20 | 658.37 |
| 1770-71 | 447.5 | 433 | £2.28 | 727.5 |
| 1771-72 | 476 | 457.5 | £2.32 | 714.12 |
| 1772-73 | 439 + 30.5 | 496.5 | £2.26 | 721.12 |
| 1773-74 | 421 | 432.25 | £2.19 | 683.75 |
| 1774-75 | 442 | 453.5 | £2.13 | 693.5 |
| 1775-76 | 449.5 + 15.5 | 481 | £2.06 | 760.87 |
| 1776-77 | 427 | 439 | £1.85 | 589.37 |
| 1777-78 | 521 | 523.25 | £1.88 | 799.12 |
| 1778-79 | 495 + 14 | 439 | £1.87 | 810.87 |
| 1779-80 | 507.5 | 492 | £1.96 | 843.62 |
| 1780-81 | 524 + 9.5 | 448.75 | £2.00 | 840.75 |
| 1781-82 | 551.5 | 463.25 | £1.97 | 913.5 |
| 1782-83 | 560 + 9 | 533.25 | £2.08 | 947.5 |
| 1783-84 | 616 | 481.25 | £2.03 | 963.25 |
| 1784-85 | 566 + 12 | 458.25 | £1.85 | 918.25 |
| 1785-86 | 373 + 15 | 612.75 | £1.72 | 617.5 |
| 1786-87 | 565.5 | 375.75 | £1.70 | 922 |
| 1787-88 | 459.5 + 16 | 535.25 | £1.67 | 784.37 |
| 1788-89 | 555.5 | 569 | £1.74 | 893.87 |
| 1789-90 | 505.9 | 511 | £2.00 | 886.75 |
| 1790-91 | 454 + 10 | 486.5 | £2.12 | 767.62 |
| 1791-92 | 490.5 + 4 | 510.75 | £2.18 | 790.25 |
| 1792-93 | 511 | 526.75 | £2.21 | 932.87 |
| 1793-94 | 444.5 | 491.25 | £2.32 | 839.25 |
| 1794-95 | 390.5 + 32 | 437.5 | £2.35 | 843.62 |
| 1795-96 | 434 + 9 | 461 | £2.40 | 778.12 |

# APPENDIX THIRTEEN.

Bromford Forge - 1746-98.

| Year | Output of finery (tons) | Output of chafery (tons) | Charcoal cost per load | Charcoal used (loads) |
|---|---|---|---|---|
| L.1746-47 | 33 | 72 | £1.50 | 66.5 |
| 1747-48 | 281 | 281.7 | £1.74 | 431.25 |
| 1748-49 | 286 + 18.5 | 308.95 | £1.74 | 428.6 |
| 1749-50 | 322.5 | 337.75 | £1.75 | 439.25 |
| 1750-51 | 298 | 329.25 | £1.71 | 422.33 |
| 1751-52 | 311.5 + 22 | 360.15 | £1.80 | 520.4 |
| 1752-53 | 340 | 346.75 | £1.89 | 532.83 |
| 1753-54 | 323 + 17 | 331.8 | £1.86 | 502.16 |
| 1754-55 | 360.5 | 389 | £1.95 | 565.5 |
| 1755-56 | 316 + 18 | 348.8 | £2.12 | 508.8 |
| 1756-57 | 335 | 341.75 | £2.27 | 506.5 |
| 1757-58 | 349.5 + 16.5 | 369.45 | £2.28 | 545.5 |
| 1758-59 | 359 | 378.25 | £2.08 | 541 |
| 1759-60 | 345.5 | 356.35 | £2.09 | 536.8 |
| 1760-61 | 304 + 31 | 345 | £2.14 | 536.16 |
| 1761-62 | 338 | 313 | £2.15 | 520.33 |
| 1762-63 | 282.5 + 20.5 | 344.25 | £1.95 | 495.5 |
| 1763-64 | 392.95 | 403.6 | £1.83 | 619.8 |
| 1764-65 | 372.5 | 386.8 | £2.01 | 516.5 |
| 1765-66 | 312.5 + 29 | 352 | £2.15 | 521 |
| 1766-67 | 366.5 | 374.6 | £2.08 | 577.66 |
| 1767-68 | 332.5 | 333.9 | £2.09 | 507.6 |
| 1768-69 | 363.5 + 22 | 407 | £2.09 | 572.6 |
| 1769-70 | 373.5 | 383 | £2.16 | 578.6 |
| 1770-71 | 365.5 | 364.75 | £2.15 | 492.33 |
| 1771-72 | 383.5 | 384.65 | £2.20 | 598 |
| 1772-73 | 334 + 36.5 | 403.75 | £2.18 | 568.25 |

| Year | Output of finery (tons) | Output of chafery (tons) | Charcoal cost per load | Charcoal used (loads) |
|---|---|---|---|---|
| 1773-74 | 336 | 344.9 | £2.08 | 522.25 |
| 1774-75 | 386 | 398 | £1.93 | 581.16 |
| 1775-76 | 373+6 | 385.4 | £1.77 | 585.33 |
| 1776-77 | 358 | 373.5 | £1.76 | 544.33 |
| 1777-78 | 395 | 376.15 | £1.82 | 593.4 |
| 1778-79 | 357+18.5 | 364.5 | £1.84 | 572 |
| 1779-80 | 363.5 | 332.75 | £1.71 | 544.83 |
| 1780-81 | 364 | 384.9 | £1.68 | 523.49 |
| 1781-82 | 366.5 | 378.7 | £1.70 | 549.33 |
| 1782-83 | 338.5+21 | 435.75 | £1.91 | 427.4 |
| 1783-84 | 348.5 | 327.5 | £1.83 | 523.4 |
| 1784-85 | 363+17 | 370.55 | £1.76 | 578.4 |
| 1785-86 | 310+15 | 315.7 | £1.66 | 493 |
| 1786-87 | 327+15 | 421.4 | £1.63 | 520.16 |
| 1787-88 | 330+11.5 | 377.65 | £1.51 | 617 |
| 1788-89 | 316.5+14 | 327.85 | £1.54 | 497 |
| 1789-90 | 320.5+16 | 357.2 | £1.69 | 513 |
| 1790-91 | 331+12 | 348 | £1.83 | 520.16 |
| 1791-92 | 308 | 317.5 | £1.88 | 462 |
| 1792-93 | 334.5 | 350.75 | £2.12 | 509.83 |
| 1793-94 | 307+22 | 339 | £2.26 | 524.33 |
| 1794-95 | 327.5 | 325.5 | £2.10 | 514.33 |
| 1795-96 | 319+22 | 348.55 | £2.10 | 562.6 |
| 1796-97 | 356+5 | 364.45 | £2.06 | 540.6 |
| 1797-98 | 311 | 334.25 | £1.93 | 426.4 |

# APPENDIX FOURTEEN.

The cost of a Ton of Iron Supplied by Hanbury of Pontypool to the Stour Partnership, 1737-1757(6).

| Year | Cost |
|---|---|
| L.1737-38 | £5.95 |
| 1738-39 | £5.94 |
| 1739-40 | £5.69 |
| 1740-41 | £5.68 |
| 1741-42 | £5.71 |
| 1742-43 | £5.71 |
| 1743-44 | £5.28 |
| 1744-45 | £5.23 |
| 1745-46 | £5.28 |
| 1746-47 | £5.25 |
| 1747-48 | £5.71 |
| 1748-49 | £6.06 |
| 1749-50 | £5.61 |
| 1750-51 | £5.78 |
| 1751-52 | £5.70 |
| 1752-53 | £5.79 |
| 1753-54 | £5.92 |
| 1754-55 | £6.61 |
| 1755-56 | £7.50 |
| 1756-57 | £7.20 |

# APPENDIX FIFTEEN.

The Cost of a Ton of Coke Pig Iron Supplied to the Stour Partnership, 1754-1800.

| Year | Darby Works | - |
|---|---|---|
| L.1754-55 | £6.50 | - |
| 1755-56 | £6.54 | - |
| 1756-57 | £6.80 | - |
| 1757-58 | £6.76 | - |
| 1758-59 | £6.74 | - |
| 1759-60 | £6.29 | - |
| 1760-61 | £6.13 | - |
| 1761-62 | £6.16 | - |
| 1762-63 | £6.50 | - |
| 1763-64 | £6.50 | - |
| 1764-65 | £6.50 | - |
| 1765-66 | £6.50 | - |
| 1766-67 | £6.50 | - |
| 1767-68 | £6.50 | John Wilkinson |
| 1768-69 | £6.50 | Bradley Ironworks |
| 1769-70 | £6.50 | £6.20 |
| 1770-71 | £6.45 | £6.20 |
| 1771-72 | £6.50 | £6.20 |
| 1772-73 | £6.50 | £6.14 |
| 1773-74 | £5.86 | £5.89 |
| 1774-75 | £5.50 | £5.43 |
| 1775-76 | £5.50 | £5.42 |
| 1776-77 | £5.79 | £5.63 |
| 1777-78 | £5.83 | £5.97 |
| 1778-79 | £5.75 | £6.05 |
| 1779-80 | £5.61 | £6.05 |
| 1780-81 | £6.01 | £6.05 |

| Year | Darby Works | - |
|---|---|---|
| 1781-82 | £6.42 | £6.05 |
| 1782-83 | £6.06 | £6.05 |
| 1783-84 | £6.12 | £6.05 |
| 1784-85 | £6.37 | £6.05 |
| 1785-86 | £6.37 | £6.05 |
| 1786-87 | £5.89 | £6.05 |
| 1787-88 | £6.12 | George Parker, Tipton |
| 1788-89 | £6.12 | £5.37 |
| 1789-90 | £5.77 | £5.41 |
| 1790-91 | £5.89 | £5.42 |
| 1791-92 | £6.12 | £5.37 |
| 1792-93 | £6.14 | £5.85 |
| 1793-94 | £6.07 | £5.89 |
| 1794-95 | £5.55 | £5.48 |
| 1795-96 | £5.59 | £5.60 |
| 1796-97 | £6.12 | £5.62 |
| 1797-98 | £5.90 | - |
| 1798-99 | £5.92 | - |
| 1799-1800 | £6.23 | - |

# APPENDIX SIXTEEN.

Profits and Losses of the Stour Partnership, 1726-1808.

| Year | Hales Furnace | Aston Furnace | Total for all furnaces and forges |
|---|---|---|---|
| L.1726-27 | £409.75 | - | £1545 |
| 1727-28 | £300.7 | - | £346.55 |
| 1728-29) | - | - | £370.2 |
| 1729-30) | £420.4 | - | -£25.7 |
| 1730-31 | £15.6 | - | £705.45 |
| 1731-32 | £168.95 | - | £1780.9 |
| 1732-33 | £18.95 | - | £730.65 |
| 1733-34 | -£62.25 | - | £38.5 |
| 1734-35 | -£303 | - | £48.8 |
| 1735-36 | -£254.95 | - | £51.6 |
| 1736-37 | -£148.75 | - | £637.5 |
| 1737-38 | £220.55 | - | £914.35 |
| 1738-39 | £263.4 | - | £1050.1 |
| 1739-40 | -£405.4 | - | £1583.55 |
| 1740-41 | £307.3 | - | £4055.25 |
| 1741-42 | -£12.4 | - | £3438.6 |
| 1742-43 | £229.75 | - | £2599 |
| 1743-44 | -£157.25 | - | £1534.8 |
| 1744-45 | £308.3 | - | £4454.7 |
| 1745-46 | -£293.75 | - | £3124.25 |
| 1746-47 | £642.1 | -£94.15 | £2937.15 |
| 1747-48 | -£101.55 | £49.95 | £3532.35 |
| 1748-49 | £365.7 | -£355.3 | £3390.1 |
| 1749-50 | -£151.4 | £443.65 | £4315.35 |
| 1750-51 | £516.85 | £1118.4 | £5923.65 |
| 1751-52 | -£93.75 | £829.3 | £7076.5 |
| 1752-53 | £696.75 | £216.6 | £4809.65 |
| 1753-54 | £90.3 | £1106.25 | £8710 |

| Year | Hales Furnace | Aston Furnace | Total for all furnaces and forges |
|---|---|---|---|
| 1754-55 | £328.65 | £1539.35 | £7537.3 |
| 1755-56 | £724.55 | £417.35 | £4629.4 |
| 1756-57 | -£264.35 | £539.95 | £4194.45 |
| 1757-58 | £1024.8 | £871.35 | £6588.35 |
| 1758-59 | £711.1 | £1431.6 | £6664.7 |
| 1759-60 | -£405.6 | £226 | £6211.15 |
| 1760-61 | £362 | £176.15 | £10617.15 |
| 1761-62 | -£383.15 | -£211.7 | £4000.8 |
| 1762-63 | £509.15 | £155.7 | £2986.2 |
| 1763-64 | -£239.5 | £813.75 | £6129.15 |
| 1764-65 | £340 | -£384.15 | £5286.85 |
| 1765-66 | -£210.75 | £335.6 | £377.45 |
| 1766-67 | £379.7 | -£431.4 | £805.7 |
| 1767-68 | -£286.6 | £501.3 | £2400.65 |
| 1768-69 | -£121.6 | £506.25 | £2227.4 |
| 1769-70 | -£299.95 | -£541.8 | £283.75 |
| 1770-71 | -£259.35 | £7.3 | £550.8 |
| 1771-72 | £18.2 | -£111.55 | £2314.45 |
| 1772-73 | - | -£383.3 | £75.05 |
| 1773-74 | - | -£396 | -£786.85 |
| 1774-75 | - | -£67.5 | £963.6 |
| 1775-76 | - | -£283.9 | £2073.2 |
| 1776-77 | - | £0.75 | £2485.8 |
| 1777-78 | - | -£239.3 | £1887.8 |
| 1778-79 | - | £95.8 | £105.7 |
| 1779-80 | - | £290.35 | £2588.55 |
| 1780-81 | - | -£274.85 | £4618.9 |
| 1781-82 | - | -£273.5 | £3818 |
| 1782-83 | - | £358.85 | £1871.2 |
| 1783-84 | - | £1.4 | £5063.65 |
| 1784-85 | - | - | £4204.6 |
| 1785-86 | - | - | £1116.6 |
| 1786-87 | - | - | £2500.2 |

| Year | Hales Furnace | Aston Furnace | Total for all furnaces and forges |
|---|---|---|---|
| 1787-88 | - | - | £3116.2 |
| 1788-89 | - | - | £2619.35 |
| 1789-90 | - | - | £1152.25 |
| 1790-91 | - | - | £2043.85 |
| 1791-92 | - | - | £1379 |
| 1792-93 | - | - | £2468.45 |
| 1793-94 | - | - | £1293.7 |
| 1794-95 | - | - | -£1244.7 |
| 1795-96 | - | - | £12.85 |
| 1796-97 | - | - | £3122.8 |
| 1797-98 | - | - | £2557.7 |
| 1798-99 | - | - | £3968.95 |
| 1799-1800 | - | - | £7729.4 |
| 1800-01 | - | - | £8111.05 |
| 1801-02 | - | - | £4004.8 |
| 1802-03 | - | - | £2827.55 |
| 1803-04 | - | - | £4257.15 |
| 1804-05 | - | - | £4902.25 |
| 1805-06 | - | - | £9476.45 |
| 1806-07 | - | - | £6275.25 |
| 1807-08 | - | - | £1153.3 |

# APPENDIX SEVENTEEN.

Output and Sales from the Forges of the Stour Partnership, 1726-1808.

| Year | Output of wrought iron (tons) | Sales (tons) |
|---|---|---|
| L.1726-27 | 618.2 | - |
| 1727-28 | 414.35 | - |
| 1728-29 | 751 | - |
| 1729-30 | 629.5 | - |
| 1730-31 | 781.3 | - |
| 1731-32 | 793.05 | - |
| 1732-33 | 789.2 | - |
| 1733-34 | 829.3 | - |
| 1734-35 | 888.95 | - |
| 1735-36 | 1100.2 | 1204.8 |
| 1736-37 | 1281.95 | 1325.45 |
| 1737-38 | 1334.5 | 1313.4 |
| 1738-39 | 1285.85 | 1201.1 |
| 1739-40 | 1414.95 | 1581.55 |
| 1740-41 | 1594.4 | 1787.75 |
| 1741-42 | 1707.9 | 1571.35 |
| 1742-43 | 1702.15 | 1386.45 |
| 1743-44 | 1663.6 | 1525.15 |
| 1744-45 | 1865.65 | 2032.65 |
| 1745-46 | 1857.3 | 2086 |
| 1746-47 | 1867.9 | 2342.45 |
| 1747-48 | 1995.45 | 2175.35 |
| 1748-49 | 2032.45 | 1681.8 |
| 1749-50 | 2226.25 | 2305.55 |
| 1750-51 | 2348.75 | 2460.35 |
| 1751-52 | 2143.68 | 2070.45 |
| 1752-53 | 2023.2 | 1815.6 |

| Year | Output of wrought iron (tons) | Sales (tons) |
|---|---|---|
| 1753-54 | 2225.1 | 2464.05 |
| 1754-55 | 2199.65 | 1859.35 |
| 1755-56 | 2184.05 | 1868.45 |
| 1756-57 | 2269.45 | 2187.6 |
| 1757-58 | 2402.15 | 2581.3 |
| 1758-59 | 2351.4 | 2539.55 |
| 1759-60 | 2283.45 | 2143.3 |
| 1760-61 | 2205.7 | 2019.5 |
| 1761-62 | 2120.6 | 1805.8 |
| 1762-63 | 2111.25 | 2233.45 |
| 1763-64 | 2223 | 2242 |
| 1764-65 | 2316.8 | 1749.75 |
| 1765-66 | 2087.55 | 1637.95 |
| 1766-67 | 2115.55 | 2459.3 |
| 1767-68 | 2137 | 2393.6 |
| 1768-69 | 2228.7 | 1882.1 |
| 1769-70 | 1979.2 | 1761 |
| 1770-71 | 2011.5 | 2088.4 |
| 1771-72 | 1969.55 | 1706.6 |
| 1772-73 | 1570.1 | 1928.8 |
| 1773-74 | 1834.75 | 1809.8 |
| 1774-75 | 1995.75 | 1925.2 |
| 1775-76 | 2085.25 | 2164.25 |
| 1776-77 | 2040.35 | 1791.55 |
| 1777-78 | 2095.2 | 1981.05 |
| 1778-79 | 2044.85 | 1555.35 |
| 1779-80 | 2002.45 | 2307.7 |
| 1780-81 | 2060.65 | 1976.95 |
| 1781-82 | 2101.1 | 1552.35 |
| 1782-83 | 2250.9 | 2275 |
| 1783-84 | 2013.5 | 2629.55 |
| 1784-85 | 1961.05 | 2121.2 |
| 1785-86 | 2117.15 | 1711.45 |

| Year | Output of wrought iron (tons) | Sales (tons) |
|---|---|---|
| 1786-87 | 2095.75 | 2042.7 |
| 1787-88 | 2312.8 | 1991.9 |
| 1788-89 | 2150.1 | 2490.5 |
| 1789-90 | 2132.65 | 2379.15 |
| 1790-91 | 1966.7 | 1975.25 |
| 1791-92 | 2006 | 1897.6 |
| 1792-93 | 2156.15 | 1889.55 |
| 1793-94 | 1919.2 | 1668.2 |
| 1794-95 | 1707.25 | 1478.85 |
| 1795-96 | 1767.35 | 2174.55 |
| 1796-97 | - | 2361 |
| 1797-98 | - | 2038.9 |
| 1798-99 | - | 2474.75 |
| 1799-1800 | - | 3084.65 |
| 1800-01 | - | 2508.5 |
| 1801-02 | - | 3081.15 |
| 1802-03 | - | 3469.3 |
| 1803-04 | - | 3549.3 |
| 1804-05 | - | 3740.6 |
| 1805-06 | - | 4287.8 |
| 1806-07 | - | 3958.85 |
| 1807-08 | - | 4020.6 |

# APPENDIX EIGHTEEN.

## Charcoal Furnaces Supplying Iron to the Forges of the Stour Partnership, 1726-1810(7).

Argyle, (Kendall & Co.) 1760-63.

Abercarn, (Jos. Glover) 1765-66.

Backbarrow, (James Machell, later John Machell) 1747-50, 1756-71, 1773-86, 1791-99.

Bishopswood, (Pendrill) 1747-48, (Foley) 1748-49, (John Mynd) 1772-73, (William Partridge) 1788-1801, 1806-07. 1809-10.

Caerphilly, (Hugh Jones & Co. of Machen) 1749-54.

Carmarthen, (Morgan) 1763-67.

Carr, (Hall & Co.) 1749-50, 1753-55.

Conway, (William Bridge & Co.) 1761-63, (Kendall) 1767-71.

Cornbrook, (Thomas Botfield) 1785-88(8).

Cradley, (Kendall) 1728-29, 1734-35, 1740-47.

Cunsey, (Cotton) 1746-47, (Hall & Co.) 1749-50, 1753-55.

Doddington, (Hall & Co.) 1749-51, 1757-58, (Kendall & Co.) 1758-62.

Dovey (Bridge & Co.) 1763-64, (Kendall & Co.) 1765-67, 1796-97.

Duddon 1740-42, (Hall) 1749-50, 1753-57, (William Latham) 1773-74, 1783-86, 1792-99.

Flaxley, (Boevey) 1732-35, 1737-39, (Thomas Crawley-Boevey) 1745-46, 1751-54, 1785-86.

Grange, (Jorden) 1747-53.

Halton, (John Ayrey) 1753-81, (Samuel Routh) 1781-83.

Kidwelly, (Robert Morgan) 1743-58, 1761-63.

Leighton, (James Machell) 1748-58, 1763-64.

Llanelly, (Hanbury) 1745-47.

Lorn, (William Ford) 1755-56, 1761-64, (John Dixon) 1771-76, (George Knott) 1776-80, 1783-85, (Executors of George Knott) 1785-1800, (George Buckle) 1805-10.

Low Wood, (John Sunderland) 1761-71, 1773-74, 1777-78, (Thomas Sunderland & John Machell) 1784-87.

Lydney, (Rowland Pytt) 1760-63, (David Tanner) 1776-88, (James, John and Robert Pidcock) 1792-93.

Mearheath, (Falkner) 1728-29, (Hall & Co.) 1743-47, 1749-50.

Netherhall, (Hartley's Atkinson & Co.) 1777-80.

Newent, (Pendrill) 1733-46, 1748-49.

Newland, (George Knott) 1781-85, (Executors of George Knott) 1785-86, 1791-92, 1795-96.

Nibthwaite, (Ford) 1740-42.

Plasmadoc, (Edward Lloyd) 1744-51.

Pontypool, (Hanbury) 1737-57.

Redbrook, (Rowland Pytt) 1755-56, 1761-63, (John Partridge Jnr.) 1785-90.

Rushall, (Kendall) 1726-28.

Seaton, (Samuel and Sampson Freeth) 1771-77, (Richard Dearman & Co.) 1779-1781, 1784-89, (J.Petty Dearman) 1793-95.

Sowley, (Hall) 1734-35, 1737-38, (William Ford) 1767-71, (John Dixon) 1771-73.

Tintern, (Richard White) 1747-48, (David Tanner) 1771-72, 1779-99, (William Thompson) 1799-1800, Robert Thompson 1800-01.

Willey, (Knight & Co.) 1726-29, 1732-33.

Ynyscedwyn, (Richard Parsons) 1786-87.

# APPENDIX NINETEEN.

Coke Furnaces Supplying Iron to the Forges of the Stour Partnership, 1754-1805.

Apedale, (G.Parker & Co.) 1788-89.

Benthall, (Banks & Onions) 1778-81, 1785-86, 1797-98, (F.B.Harries & Co.) 1802-1804.

Bilston, (John Wilkinson) 1759-60, (William Bickley & Co.) 1789-91, 1794-1801, (Fereday & Turton) 1801-02.

Blaenavon, (Thomas Hill & Co.) 1791-92, 1796-97, 1800-04.

Bradley, (John Wilkinson) 1768-87.

Brierley, (Seager & Co.) 1799-1800.

Broseley, (Banks & Onions) 1788-89, 1791-93, 1798-99, 1801-02, (John Onions) 1803-04.

Calcutts, (George Matthews) 1771-72, 1774-78, (Matthews & Homfray) 1778-79, (George Matthews) 1784-85, (Messrs Baillie, Pocock & Co.) 1786-87.

Coalbrookdale, (Darby) 1754-55.

Cornbrook, (Thomas Botfield) 1788-94, 1798-99.

Coseley, (George Stokes & Co.) 1789-90, (Pemberton & Stokes) 1790-96.

Cyfarthfa, 1783-84, 1786-87(9).

Donnington, (Richard Dearman & Co.) 1787-88, (Bishton & Co.) 1796-1802.

Dowlais, (J.Jones & Co.) 1764-65, 1772-73.

Dudley Wood (George Attwood & Sons) 1803-05.

Gornal, (Banks & Co.) 1801-02

Gospel Oak, (Banks & Onions) 1793-94, 1796-98.

Hirwaun, (Jos. Glover & Son) 1785-88.

Horsehay & Ketley (Darby, Reynolds etc.) 1755-1805.

Level, (William Croft) 1787-88, (Messrs T.W. & B. Gibbons) 1788-90.

Lightmoor, (George Perry & Co.) 1758-84, (Francis & John Homfray) 1787-90.

Lilleshall, (John Bishton) 1802-05.

Neath Abbey, (G.C. Fox & Co.) 1797-1800.

Netherton, (George Attwood & Sons) 1802-03.

New Willey, (John Wilkinson & Co.) 1758-60, (Brooke Forester & Co.) 1765-66, (John Wilkinson) 1776-77.

Old Park, (Thomas Botfield) 1791-1805.

Park Head, (Zach. Parker) 1801-02.

Partridge Nest, (Thomas Kinnersley) 1793-94.

Plymouth, 1786-87.

Snedshill, (John Wilkinson) 1781-94, (G.Biscoe) 1797-98, (John Bishton & Co.) 1798-1804.

Silverdale, (William Sneyd) 1793-94

Tipton, (George Parker) 1781-97, (Hawks & Co.) 1801-02.

Toll End, (Richard Hawks) 1801-02.

Varteg, (Varteg Hill Iron Co.) 1802-05.

# APPENDIX TWENTY.

The Output of John Knight & Co., 1810-1828.

| Year | Refined pig iron (tons) | Iron made (tons) | Iron puddled (tons) | Tinplate (boxes) | Wire (bundles) |
|---|---|---|---|---|---|
| L.1810-11 | 1627.75 | 1212.75 | 869.5 | - | 7472 |
| 1811-12 | 3958 | 1557 | 1132.5 | - | 6166 |
| 1812-13 | 4128 | 2186.75 | 1110 | - | 7597 |
| 1813-14 | 4450 | 2590.5 | 1272.75 | - | 7431.5 |
| 1814-15 | 4138.5 | 1991.75 | 1667.5 | 1386 | 10243.25 |
| 1815-16 | 3970.75 | 2356.75 | 1212.75 | 8158 | 7943.75 |
| 1816-17 | 2389.75 | 1155.5 | 933.75 | 4315 | 5262 |
| 1817-18 | 2114.25 | 1527.25 | 1329.25 | 6203 | 8356 |
| 1818-19 | 4190.5 | 1964.75 | 1925.75 | 8869 | 9962 |
| 1819-20 | 3975.5 | 1944.75 | 1670.75 | 7649 | 8018.5 |
| 1820-21 | 4361.25 | 1952 | 1823.5 | 9189 | 7572 |
| 1821-22 | 4534.5 | 2070.5 | 2053.75 | 9116 | 10267 |
| 1822-23 | 4703.25 | 1759.25 | 2345.25 | 9466 | 7740 |
| 1823-24 | 5304.5 | 1523.5 | 3433 | 14412 | C.7000 |
| 1824-25 | 5816.25 | 2094.25 | 3331 | 14177 | 8711 |
| 1825-26 | 5154 | 1837.5 | 2985.75 | 11828 | 8451 |
| 1826-27 | 5345.25 | 1934.75 | 3024 | 15108 | 7290 |
| 1827-28 | 6071.75 | 2092.75 | 3188.25 | 19060 | 7947 |

# APPENDIX TWENTY ONE.

The Output of John Knight & Co., 1829-50.

| Year | Refined pigs (tons) | Charcoal iron (tons) | Coke iron made (tons) | Iron puddled (tons) | Tinplate (boxes) | Wire (bundles) |
|---|---|---|---|---|---|---|
| 1828-29 | 5960 | 1965.75 | 97.75 | 2537 | 18595 | 6533 |
| 1829-30 | 5051.75 | 1368 | 568.25 | 3108.75 | 15219 | 5406 |
| 1830-31 | 5970.75 | 1310.5 | 958.25 | 3141.5 | 18605 | 7796 |
| 1831-32 | 5546 | 1289.75 | 947.75 | 3128.75 | 16017 | 7543 |
| 1832-33 | 5844.75 | 1479.75 | 1015.25 | 3985.75 | 17078 | 7067 |
| 1833-34 | 6156.75 | 1741.75 | 844.75 | 3233 | 19243 | 7868 |
| 1834-35 | 6334.5 | 1829.5 | 898.75 | 3393.5 | 19679 | 8460 |
| 1835-36 | 6953 | 2120.25 | 578 | 3677.5 | 20066 | 8663 |
| 1836-37 | 6499.75 | 2446.75 | 374.25 | 3317.25 | 17574 | 9041 |
| 1837-38 | 6112.5 | 2062.75 | 501 | 3569.25 | 16981 | 8894 |
| 1838-39 | 7719 | 2555.25 | 610.5 | 4590.5 | 19376 | 9553 |
| 1839-40 | 7469.25 | 2449.25 | 501.75 | 4045 | 16403 | 9931 |
| 1840-41 | 7405.5 | 2098.75 | 622 | 4545.25 | 20941 | 11242 |
| 1841-42 | 7295 | 2274.5 | 492.25 | 4000 | 19446 | 10470 |
| 1842-43 | 5829.75 | 2137.5 | 637.5 | 3465.25 | 17581 | 6655 |
| 1843-44 | 5857.5 | 2400 | 447.75 | 3742.25 | 20354 | 6927 |
| 1844-45 | 5944.25 | 2337 | 697.25 | 4101.5 | 21029 | 7109 |
| 1845-46 | 6549.25 | 2189 | 866 | 4261.25 | 19778 | 5142 |
| 1846-47 | 5704.5 | 2263 | 479.25 | 4077.75 | 17073 | 4482 |
| 1847-48 | 5255 | 2049.25 | 588.5 | 4044.25 | 13768 | 4559 |
| 1848-49 | 5870.5 | 2279.25 | 500 | 4740 | 18299 | 7664 |
| 1849-50 | 5868.25 | 2213.75 | 684.5 | 4369 | 20379 | 8104 |

# APPENDIX TWENTY TWO.

John Knight & Co. : Sales and Profits, 1810-1850.

| Year | Charcoal cost per load | Iron sold (tons) | Tinplate sold (boxes) | Wire sold (bundles) | Profit/ loss |
|---|---|---|---|---|---|
| 1810-11 | - | 2210.3 | - | 7287 | £2547.8 |
| 1811-12 | - | 2157.1 | - | 5172 | -£327.75 |
| 1812-13 | - | 2580 | - | 7162 | £10050.15 |
| 1813-14 | - | 3286.15 | - | 8559 | £12697.6 |
| 1814-15 | £3.11 | 2601.3 | 1026 | 8830 | £6350.25 |
| 1815-16 | £3.19 | 2042.6 | 8383 | 7837 | £4092.6 |
| 1816-17 | £2.49 | 1401.75 | 4057.5 | 5903 | £497.35 |
| 1817-18 | £2.30 | 1821.9 | 7132 | 8756 | £5822.55 |
| 1818-19 | £2.66 | 2480.6 | 8770 | 10147 | £10075.1 |
| 1819-20 | £3.03 | 2211.7 | 6876 | 7801 | £4329.25 |
| 1820-21 | £2.80 | 2423.9 | 9266 | 7878 | £3352.55 |
| 1821-22 | £2.77 | 2434.25 | 10150 | 9662 | £4112.8 |
| 1822-23 | £2.61 | 2791.7 | 9617 | 8215 | £7321.5 |
| 1823-24 | £2.87 | 3312.75 | 11388 | 6724 | £8745.85 |
| 1824-25 | £3.01 | 3159.85 | 13324 | 7303 | £16179 |
| 1825-26 | £2.88 | 3232.55 | 12281 | 8188 | £10685.7 |
| 1826-27 | £2.91 | 3027.35 | 13458 | 7526.3 | £10296.25 |
| 1827-28 | £2.79 | 3353.55 | 19511 | 7907 | £13641 |
| 1828-29 | £2.76 | 3515 | 16150 | 6212 | £9275 |
| 1829-30 | £2.79 | 3384.15 | 14456 | 5406 | £8704 |
| 1830-31 | £2.93 | 3322.2 | 18343 | 7806 | £12864 |
| 1831-32 | £3.03 | 3483.4 | 18265 | 7388 | £8099.15 |
| 1832-33 | £2.90 | 3583.3 | 16776 | 7233 | £8513.45 |
| 1833-34 | £2.87 | 3555 | 21831.5 | 7955 | £15341.7 |
| 1834-35 | £2.86 | 3576.95 | 18892 | 8414.5 | £15135.45 |
| 1835-36 | £2.68 | 4158.95 | 22902 | 9278.5 | £19782 |
| 1836-37 | £2.56 | 3762.9 | 15076 | 9497.5 | £13113.15 |

| Year | Charcoal cost per load | Iron sold (tons) | Tinplate sold (boxes) | Wire sold (bundles) | Profit/ loss |
|---|---|---|---|---|---|
| 1837-38 | £2.77 | 3993.5 | 18955 | 8943 | £15005.5 |
| 1838-39 | £2.76 | 5109.35 | 20168 | 9239 | £20709.5 |
| 1839-40 | £2.88 | 4620.85 | 15586 | 10122.5 | £18012.65 |
| 1840-41 | £3.01 | 4350.85 | 21716 | 11555 | £18221.3 |
| 1841-42 | £2.87 | 4125.95 | 19724 | 10704 | £11146.1 |
| 1842-43 | £2.73 | 3623.7 | 16395 | 7492 | £7104.8 |
| 1843-44 | £2.66 | 4135.6 | 21127 | 7111 | £10697.7 |
| 1844-45 | £2.57 | 4507.2 | 21130 | 7233 | £18518.7 |
| 1845-46 | £2.57 | 4530 | 18631 | 5037 | £15492.4 |
| 1846-47 | £2.55 | 4371.15 | 17531 | 4590 | £8554.4 |
| 1847-48 | £2.60 | 4674.55 | 14587 | 4465 | £2481.9 |
| 1848-49 | £2.51 | 4701.65 | 18298 | 7701 | £9815.35 |
| 1849-50 | £2.42 | 4605 | 20452 | 7903 | £12635 |

# BIBLIOGRAPHY.

## Manuscript Sources.

Kidderminster Public Library: Knight Manuscripts, consisting of letters, leases, papers and the accounts of the Stour Partnership and Bringewood Partnership. While preparing this volume the Knight Manuscripts were moved to their new home at Worcester County Record Office.

Birmingham Reference Library: Boulton & Watt Collection, lists of ironworks

Gwent County Record Office, Cwmbran: Mr. Hanbury's Cost and Yields of Pig, Rod, Hoop and Sheet Iron.

Worcestershire Record Office, Worcester: Articles of Agreement, 18th March 1709.

Herefordshire Record Office, Hereford: Downton Castle Papers.

## Printed Material.

H.G.Bull, Some Account of Bringewood Forge and Furnace, Transactions of the Woolhope Naturalists' Field Club, 1869.

Betty Caswell, A Scrapbook of Cookley Memories, Cookley,1989.

R.H.Campbell, Carron Company, Edinburgh, 1961.

R.L.Downes, The Stour Partnership 1726-36, Economic History Review, 2nd series, 3, 1950

The Engineer.

Oliver Fairclough, The Grand Old Mansion : The Holtes and their Successors at Aston Hall, 1618-1864, Birmingham, 1984.

W.K.V.Gale, The Black Country Iron Industry, 1979.

W.H.Greenwood, A Manual of Metallurgy, Vol 1, 1886.

G.Hammersley, The Charcoal Iron Industry and its Fuel 1540-1750, Economic History Review, 2nd series, 26, 1973.

J.R.Harris, The British Iron Industry, 1700-1850, 1988.

C.K.Hyde, Technological Change in the British Iron Industry, 1700-1870, Princeton, 1977.

C.K.Hyde, The Iron Industry in the West Midlands in 1754 : Observations from the Travel Diary of Charles Wood, West Midlands Studies, Vol 6, 1973.

E.W.Hulme, Statistical History of the Iron Trade of England and Wales 1717-50, Transactions of the Newcomen Society, 9 , 1928-29.

Elizabeth Inglis-Jones, The Knights of Downton Castle, The National Library of Wales Journal, Vol XV, No. 3, 1968.

B.L.C.Johnson, The Foley Partnerships: The Iron Industry at the End of the Charcoal Era, Economic History Review, series 2, 4 (3), 1952

B.L.C.Johnson, New Light on the Iron Industry of the Forest of Dean, Transactions of the Bristol and Gloucestershire Archaeological Society, 1953.

Peter W. King, Wolverley Lower Mill and the Beginnings of the Tinplate Industry, Historical Metallurgy, Vol 22, No. 2, 1988.

Rachel Labouchere, Abiah Darby, York, 1988.

R.A.Lewis, Two Partnerships of the Knights - A Study of the Midland Iron Industry in the Eighteenth Century, M.A. Thesis, Birmingham University, 1949.

W.E.Minchinton, The British Tinplate Industry - A History, Oxford, 1957.

R.A.Mott, Abraham Darby I and II and the Coal Iron Industry, Transactions of the Newcomen Society, Vol. 31, 1957-58.

R.A.Mott, (Ed. P.Singer), Henry Cort : The Great Finer, 1983.

Norman Mutton, Charlcot Furnace 1773-1779, Historical Metallurgy Group Bulletin, 1966.

Nash, History of Worcestershire, II,1799.

C.S.Orwin & R.J.Sellick, The Reclamation of Exmoor Forest, Newton Abbot, 1970.

Alex den Ouden, The Production of Wrought Iron in Finery Hearths, Part One, Journal of the Historical Metallurgy Society, Vol. 15, No. 2, 1981.

R.Page, Richard and Edward Knight; Ironmasters of Bringewood and Wolverley, Transactions of the Woolhope Naturalists' Field Club, 43, 1981

Marie B. Rowlands, Masters and Men in the West Midlands Metalware Trades Before the Industrial Revolution, Manchester, 1975.

Philip Riden, A Gazeteer of Charcoal-fired Blast Furnaces in Great Britain in use since 1660, Cardiff, 1987.

H.R.Schubert, History of the British Iron and Steel Industry fom C450 B.C. to A.D. 1775, 1957

L.J.Thompson, Guide to Cookley and Wolverley, 1902.

Barrie Trinder, The Industrial Revolution in Shropshire, Chichester, 1973.

# NOTES AND REFERENCES FOR THE APPENDICES.

1. The Bringewood accounts start with figures for the period Midsummer 1733 to Ladyday 1734 and then they are yearly accounts stretching from one Ladyday to the next Ladyday.

2. The Charlcotte Furnace accounts commence with a two year period and then are yearly Ladyday accounts.

3. The Hales Furnace was hardly in blast during L.1728-29 and so the figures were added to the next year's accounts.

4. The figures here would indicate that the forge was not in operation for the full year.

5. Not in operation for the full year.

6. These are the figures for the purchase of iron at the works without any of the transport costs added.

7. For the background history of many of these furnaces see, Philip Riden, *A Gazetteer of Charcoal-fired Blast Furnaces in Great Britain in use since 1660*, Cardiff, 1987.

8. Cornbrook was a unique furnace in the context of the Knight accounts for it seems to have started production as a charcoal fired furnace and then to have changed over to using coke as a fuel in 1788. In L.1787-88 a ton of charcoal iron from Cornbrook cost £8.20 and in the next year Cornbrook was producing coke iron for sale at £5.50 per ton which gives an indication of the savings that could be made through the use of mineral fuel.

9. The Cyfarthfa iron was supplied by the Homfray family but they did not own the furnace. The Homfrays leased the cannon boring mill next to the furnace but part of the agreement stipulated that they buy pig iron from Cyfarthfa.

# Index